HEART OF THE HOME

COPYRIGHT 2000

FIRST PRINTING & COPYRIGHT 1995

3RD PRINTING

THIS MATERIAL MAY NOT BE

DUPLICATED IN ANY MANNER

WITHOUT WRITTEN CONSENT FROM THE COPY-

RIGHT HOLDER

ISBN # 0-9654336-0-9

BY ANN JACKSON

DESIGN BY JULIE BELCHER
YEE-HAW INDUSTRIES

00-045424

HEART *of the* HOME

By Ann Jackson

"IF YOU ARE CAREFUL," GARP WROTE, "IF YOU USE GOOD INGREDIENTS, AND YOU DON'T TAKE ANY SHORTCUTS, THEN YOU CAN USUALLY COOK SOMETHING VERY GOOD. SOMETIMES IT'S THE ONLY WORTHWHILE PRODUCT YOU CAN SALVAGE FROM A DAY: WHAT YOU MAKE TO EAT. WITH WRITING, I FIND, YOU CAN HAVE ALL THE RIGHT INGREDIENTS, GIVE PLENTY OF TIME AND CARE, AND STILL GET NOTHING. ALSO TRUE OF LOVE. COOKING, THEREFORE, CAN KEEP A PERSON WHO TRIES HARD SANE."

— JOHN IRVING

TO MY GRANDMOTHERS

HAVIN' FUN WASHIN' DISHES

Why can't vegetarians still have mashed potatoes and gravy? Why did "Health Desserts" always taste like the main ingredient was dirt? Why was it that now that I was a vegetarian I was doomed to a life of "topped with alfalfa sprouts" and dinner out meant always having to order eggplant parmesan? Did throwing the fried chicken out the window mean the gravy had to go to? Why did vegetarians have the reputation of being passive, mellow and tame; the way I cooked was radical and the most exciting part of the day. I felt misunderstood.

You can be healthy and I do mean dairyless and it doesn't have to be boring. Why does that word have to be so scary?? Dairyless. Let's face it, everyone who cares anything about their body has faced the music and given up dairy products. The experts all say the same thing; No Dairy! When I stopped eating dairy products I dropped twenty pounds and I've never gained it back, not to this day, and it has been years.

I had never been able to completely control my weight. You know the syndrome; lose fifteen pounds, look great and before you know it, you can't get your pants zipped up. Yeah, sure, sometimes I would get skinny, but it was usually because I got sick, or fell in love; something totally accidental. It was like I had this layer of baby fat that I just couldn't get rid of. At least not permanently.

Before I went dairyless I thought, this can't be that much different. I don't eat much cheese, do I? You guessed it... I couldn't think of anything to eat. I lived on popcorn for days! I realized that I was as much into the cow as I had ever been. Every cookbook I looked in (even the hip vegetarian ones) had recipes that featured two kinds of cheese, milk, and butter. I felt obsessed- visions of a grassy knoll and a book depository. I could ramble on for hours at this point on my dairyless decision... the disappearance of my double chin, all my neck wrinkles going away, never being constipated anymore, my skin turning soft as silk (not milk), no more colds caught every time one came along, and no more sour milk breath. After all, it's my double chin we're talking about here!

I didn't change any other part of my diet. I tried to supplement my diet with seaweed whenever I could. One serving of seaweed has fourteen times more calcium than a glass of milk. Seaweed? Sound pretty strict?? What about Japanese Pearl Divers?? These women dive to considerable depths, naked, almost every day until they are in their seventies. They have beautiful long shiny hair and strong fingernails. What do they make it a point to eat every day? Seaweed.

If you are a little over weight, chronically constipated, need to lower your cholesterol level, have skin problems or gas problems, allergy problems, or if you wake up in the morning, all mucoused out, hacking and spitting like crazy- you are dairyed out. Try these dairyless recipes, you will see results, major results in three to four weeks. I felt a new kind of independence, like when I quit cigarettes.

I am not trying to push any kind of special diet. I do not pretend to be an expert at anything, especially cooking, but I do know what works for me. I did have a job cooking for thirty-seven picky vegetarian men and I got to know what they liked too. What good is it how healthy something is if it doesn't taste good?

These recipes tend to be simple, straight-forward, and hard to mess up. Most ingredients can be gotten at your grocery store or health food store. If you can't find them, fake it! You don't have to follow the recipe exactly; I encourage you to experiment. If you don't want to use soy milk, fine, use milk, use cream for all I care (they're your thighs)- just get in there and do it! Don't let the kitchen intimidate you. Don't think of yourself as the kind of person who doesn't know how to cook. Buy a few mixing bowls, make the kitchen a nice place to be, and you'll find yourself spending more time there. It's really the best room in the house, isn't it? The best adventures start there. The most romantic dates usually end up there (I've met some of the most remarkable people by the light of the refrigerator door).

And now girls, on a lighter note. Yes, it is really true, "The way to a man's heart is through his stomach." If you are having man trouble, married or single, sixteen or sixty, or if you have spent one too many lonely, boring weekends, then girl, get with it. Get in that kitchen and make a pineapple-upside-down cake. Rattle some pots and pans. You won't be surprised at the results, you will be shocked. Give a little of yourself, what's the big thing?? Find out what his "favorite foods" are and make them for him. Wear a little apron. There are African tribes that believe if a woman cooks one meal for a man, he is tied to her for life. Think what a weeks worth of fried chicken tofu, mashed potatoes with gravy, and ginger bread could do. You will be rewarded a hundred fold. If you don't have a man, fine, find a friend; no one can resist a nice cozy kitchen.

It really is a magical place, the kitchen. There is something there for everyone, full of cupboards for those of us who need a little security, a refuge for those of us who are weary and weak from slugging it out in the world. It is a chance to stir obsessively, to clean-up, to mess up. It's a chance to know what nourishes you from A to Z because you put it there. It is a chance to see your effort manifest, not only in yourself, but in those you love. It is the chance to reap the fruits of your labor.
It is the chance to be rewarded every day with big shining eyes and heartfelt kisses. It is the chance to have the good, deep-down feeling of doing something correctly, thoroughly, and completely. It is the chance to feel positive and strong about your life. It is the chance to put a heart into your home.

Ann Jackson

HEART
of the
HOME

TABLE of CONTENTS

SALADS

Potato Salad

Tabouli Salad

Crab Ralph

Addicting Tempeh Chicken Salad

Tofu Egg Salad

The Best Marinated Salad

Pasta Salad

Cole Slaw

DRESSINGS

Vinaigrette

The House Special

Wee Blu Inn Salad Dressing

Tahini Lemon Dressing

Basic Marinade

Lindsey's Good On A Hot Day Salad Dressing

Tofu Mayonnaise

How To Toast/Roast Nuts

Hell No, We Won't Glow Salad Dressing

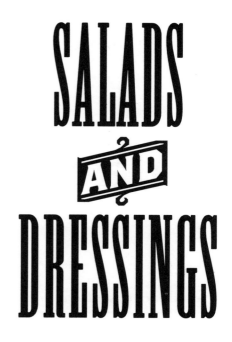

SALADS AND DRESSINGS

"LET ONION ATOMS LURK
WITHIN THE BOWL AND,
HALF SUSPECTED,
ANIMATE THE WHOLE."
SIDNEY SMITH 1771-1845
RECIPE FOR A SALAD

Potato Salad

5 or 6 big potatoes (red skinned are best)
1 onion
3 or 4 stalks celery, with leaves
1/4 tsp. garlic powder
1 scant tsp. dill weed
salt and pepper to taste
a little about 2 tbs. of the juice poured off the top of a jar of pickles
1/2 to 1 cup of mayonnaise
(if you are a dairy eater, put in half sour cream half mayo)
1/4 tsp. turmeric (optional)
1/4 chopped parsley
1 to 2 tbs Dijon mustard
1 tbs. poppyseeds
2-3 hard boiled eggs chopped - if you eat eggs

The secret of this salad is to mix it when hot, and then let it sit awhile in the refrigerator.

Boil the potatoes whole with the skins left on. Chop them up into a big bowl. Grate about 1/4 of the onion right into the bowl. Chop up the rest of the onion and add to the mixture along with the chopped celery and rest of the ingredients. Stir this up well. It's best when left in the refrigerator overnight, but 4 or 5 hours should be enough time to cool it off if you are pressed.

This salad is so good; lots of people tell me it's the best they've ever had. At potlucks or covered dish suppers, a crowd tends to form around the potato salad and you hear exclamations of "why, home made potato salad, I haven't had that in years!"

P.S. After rereading this I see I forgot to mention salt. In this recipe you do not want to forget it as I think it needs a lot. I usually put in a good shake right after I cut up the potatoes and add a little more when I begin stirring it all up. I usually have to taste this several times to adjust. Remember when you are tasting it that after it sits awhile it starts to taste better.

Tabouli Salad

1 cup bulgar
3/4 cup olive oil
3/4 cup lemon juice
1/2 cup chopped green onions
1/4 cup fresh peppermint leaves, chopped
(if you must use dried, use about 1 tbs.
1 bunch parsley, chopped fine
1 cup black olives
2 cups tomatoes, chopped
1 cucumber, diced
salt and pepper to taste

Soak bulgar in double the amount of water until it is completely absorbed (about an hour). Chop all the vegetables and add to the bulgar, along with the peppermint, oil, and lemon juice. Mix this well and salt to taste. Serve very cold with hummus, falafel, or baba ganoush.

I like tabouli a lot, but I don't like it unless it is made with lots of stuff in it like this. Plain, it just doesn't do much for me, but with cucumbers, tomatoes, and olives, it is a real summer time treat. If I am feeling really fancy, or am having friends over for middle eastern food, I add little chunks of feta cheese to the salad.

CRAB RALPH

This recipe was discovered by accident when Lindsey spaced-out and left three pallets of mushrooms outside, overnight. We sold most of them off for cheap, I made stuffed mushrooms, cream of mushroom soup, and this wild salad of marinated mushrooms, artichoke hearts, and red onion rings, but there were still a lot left that were beginning to get those funky brown spots. (I know this sounds weird, but CRAB RALPH tastes best when mushrooms are like this, one day from being thrown away.) So, Ralph, a true produce man at heart who lives by the motto "Sell it or smell it" offered to give it a try. We all loved what he made and thought it tasted like crab. Here's what he did:

2 to 3 cups mushrooms, whole
(when ready for salad chop very fine)
1 big spoonful of mayonnaise or sour cream substitute
1/2 TBS. kelp powder
1/2 TBS. dijon mustard
1/2 TBS. poppyseeds
juice of half lemon
1/2 small onion, grated or chopped fine
1/2 cup celery chopped up
salt and pepper
pinch of Old Bay Seasonings (optional)

Combine all ingredients in a big bowl. Add more mayo if you need to. Adjust to your liking. Serve immediately. Best stuffed into avocados or tomatoes, or even on dark bread with Bloody Mary's.

13

ADDICTING TEMPEH CHICKEN SALAD

1 block tempeh
1/2 to 3/4 cup mayonnaise
depending on how much you like
1/2 large onion, chopped
(or a few green onions)
1/2 cup celery including leaves, chopped fine
(or 1 tsp. celery seed)
2 to 3 TBS. good tasting nutritional yeast
1/2 tsp. salt
grated black pepper
chopped tomatoes (optional)

Steam the tempeh lightly for about 25 minutes. Chop into chunks and put into bowl with the rest of the ingredients. Grate as much of the onion as you can and when it gets to your eyes badly chop the rest.

Refrigerate and when chilled it's ready.

This is a recipe that sounds just so-so. When I heard steamed tempeh I thought, "Yuck!" But then I tried it..When I called this addicting, I wasn't kidding. It is completely delicious. It's good in avocados, tomatoes, sandwiches, and more. I have made this and eaten the whole thing before it even got to the fridg. It is also good in tacos or burritos or as a chip dip. Please try this one. Here's a tip. Just do this the way you remember making tuna or chicken salad.

Tofu Egg Salad

1 block tofu
1 stick celery, chopped fine
1/2 onion
1 TBS. good tasting nutritional yeast
1 tsp. poppyseeds
1 tsp. dijon mustard
1/4 tsp. dill weed
1/4 cup mayonnaise
1/2 tsp. turmeric
salt and pepper to taste

Mash the tofu in a bowl. Add the celery and the rest of the ingredients and mix well. Add the turmeric a little at a time until the salad is the color you like (this is sometimes called imitation egg salad).

P.S. Grate as much of the onion as you can, until your eyes start to water unbearably... then just chop the rest. If you have any pickles in the fridge, pour off just a little of the juice into the salad. This should about do it.

THE BEST MARINATED SALAD

Use three or more of the following ingredients. Don't feel like you must use them all. The beauty of this salad is that it's just as good with a few items as with a lot. And it's so easy.

LAYER IN A LARGE SALAD BOWL:

Avocados, chopped
Red onions, sliced in rings
Green onions
Olives, black or green
Asparagus Tips
Alfalfa Sprouts
Feta or Blue Cheese, cubed or crumbled
Tomatoes are good but add before serving— they'll get soggy
Mushrooms, sliced
Artichoke Hearts
Pimentos - or red peppers
Corn, cut off the cob
Steamed Tempeh, cubed
Parsley, finely chopped
Cucumbers, peeled and sliced
Roasted garlic

Now add the dressing. Almost any oil and lemon dressing will do.

HERE'S A GOOD ONE:

2/3 cup olive oil
1/4 cup lemon juice or rice vinegar or balsamic vinegar
1 tsp. dry mustard or 2 tsp. dijon mustard
2 cloves garlic, smashed
1 TBS. fresh basil (1/2 tsp. dried) or oregano
salt and pepper to taste

Put it all in the blender and mix well, then pour over the top of your layered salad. Barely toss and put in the refrigerator for a few hours. Before serving, toss again.

PASTA SALAD

5 to 6 cups cooked pasta
(You want nice al dente noodles for this, nothing remotely mushy. I like plain old white noodles or either buckwheat noodles. There's a kind called Jinenjo that are great. Another very light, thin noodle is called cellophane noodles. You can find these in the oriental section of your supermarket.)

1/2 cup oil and vinegar dressing
1 TBS. umboushi paste
2 tsp. dry mustard
1 pinch nutmeg
2 cups steamed asparagus stalks and tips
1/2 cup chopped green onions
1/2 cup chopped fresh parsley
1/4 cup sour cream (optional)
juice of 1/2 lemon
generous salt and pepper
2 tomatoes, diced
1 to 2 cups snow peas, lightly steamed
1/2 to 1 cup toasted, sliced almonds or walnuts
1 Package of your favorite pasta

Mix well in a bowl: the dressing, umboushi paste, nutmeg, mustard, lemon, sour cream, salt, and pepper. When well mixed, add to freshly cooked hot pasta (when the noodles are hot they absorb more of the flavors). Next, gently toss in the asparagus, peas, green onions, and parsley. Refrigerate until well chilled. Toss in the tomatoes and nuts just before serving. This is a great light salad, perfect for dinner on a hot summer night with a tall glass of iced tea. It is very elegant and in no way resembles the macaroni salad from the school cafeteria.

P.S. You can substitute artichoke hearts for the asparagus when it's out of season or if you don't have any around.

Cole Slaw

Is there anything easier than cole slaw?? Or better tasting? It is the perfect bite to take after a hot buttery hushpuppy. Cool, sweet, and crunchy... what else could sit on a plate of barbecue and fit in so well? I never went to a backyard picnic that did not have cole slaw. Here's how I do it:

1 medium head cabbage
1/2 to 3/4 cup mayonnaise
1 tsp. poppyseeds
juice of 1/2 lemon
plenty of salt and black pepper
1 pinch sugar
1/2 small onion, grated (optional)
1 small carrot, grated (optional)

Slice the cabbage **finely**. Mix the other ingredients together in a measuring cup. Pour over cabbage and toss. Cover and keep in fridge for about an hour or until ready to eat.

Vinaigarette Dressing

This is the base for most of the salad dressings I make. I use 3 parts of oil to 1 part lemon juice or vinegar. Be free with your imagination... olive oil is always good, yet so are sesame and safflower. Instead of lemon juice try lime, or instead of rice vinegar, red wine or tarragon vinegar or balsamic.

The list of things you can try in salad dressing is almost endless: miso, chili sauce, ketchup, kelp powder, ecetera... tofu or avocado can be used as thickeners. Go to your window sill and pick a few herbs; dill and basil will do wonders (don't use fresh herbs unless you're serving the dressing immediately; they get too strong if left to sit).

HERE'S THE RECIPE:

2/3 cup oil (olive is my favorite)
1/4 to 1/3 cup lemon juice or vinegar
2 cloves garlic
2 tsp. dry mustard or grey poupon
dash of salt
generous grind of fresh black pepper

Combine the ingedients in a blender or a jar with lid, and mix well. Keep in a cold place until ready to use, then give it a shake and enjoy!

THE HOUSE SPECIAL

Most restaurants refer to their best dressing as "The House Special." Here's mine: Follow the basic Vinaigrette dressing recipe, then add 2 tsp. oregano and 2 tsp. poppyseeds. Pour into a jar with a bay leaf and give it a shake. Let it sit a couple of hours in the fridge. You can't beat this.

Wee Blu Inn Salad Dressing

2/3 cup olive or sesame oil
1/4 cup lemon juice or vinegar
2 cloves garlic, smashed
1 cup mayonnaise
(or 1/2 cup mayo and 1/2 cup sour cream)
2 tsp. oregano
1/4 to 1/2 cup blue cheese
salt and pepper to taste

Set aside half the amount of blue cheese and combine the rest of the ingredients in a blender. When smooth, remove and stir in the rest of the cheese, crumbled into pieces. This is a versatile dressing that is good over any salad. It's also unbeatable as a dip for artichokes, or even spooned over sliced tomatoes and broiled.

TAHINI LEMON DRESSING

1/4 cup tahini
juice of one or two lemons
1/2 cup water
1-2 cloves thru press
1/4 tsp. salt
1/4 tsp. cumin

Put the tahini in a small bowl. Squeeze the lemon over it and add the garlic powder and salt. Stir in water until it makes a smooth liquid, not a paste. This is the same dressing used over falafel in middle eastern restaurants.

Once when Patsy and I were hitch-hiking to Erie two mill hunks picked us up. We were hungry and had packed a lunch, so we pulled out our sandwhiches and started to eat. The guy in the passenger seat turned around and I asked him if he wanted a bite of my sandwich.

"What kind is it?" he asked suspiciously.

"It's tahini and honey with raisins on whole wheat."

Before I could eat another bite the guy grabbed my sandwich and threw it out the window. "Nobody should have to eat something like that!" he said.

I appreciated his spontaneous honesty. With nothing to drink it had been a pretty cloggy sandwich anyway... but please don't be afraid to try something new once in a while. If you didn't try new food now and then you'd still be eating pablum.

BASIC MARINADE

Marinades are really easy. You can use whatever's around. Marinated tofu, tempeh, or wheat gluten will take on most any taste quickly. It's good too for grilled vegetables. Here are a few basic marinades. Just whip it all up in a blender and pour over whatever you're marinating. Use a glass or stainless steel bowl, and refrigerate if it'll be marinating for more than an hour or so.

NO 1
1/2 cup oil
1/2 cup red wine
1 tsp. dry mustard
1 bay leaf
ground pepper to taste

NO 2
1/4 cup olive oil
3 TBS. dry vermouth
2 TBS. chopped parsley
1 tsp. dried tarragon

NO 3
1/4 cup tamari (mixed with 1/4 cup water)
2 TBS. sesame oil
1 TBS. prepared horseradish
a squeeze of lemon
1 clove garlic

NO 4
1 cup beer
dash of salt
1 TBS. dry mustard
3 TBS. tamari
2 cloves garlic

NO 5
1/2 onion chopped & sauteed in 1/4 cup oil
1 or 2 TBS. tahini
juice of 1/2 lemon
1 tsp. oregano
1 tsp. paparika
salt and pepper

Lindsey's Good on a Hot Day Salad Dressing

My friend Lindsey used to come in the kitchen and ask, "What can I do to help?" "How about make a salad dressing," I'd always say. I had to pry this recipe out of her, and she gave it to me in "a pinch of this, a handful of that" style. It is one of the greats.

3/4 cup safflower oil
1/4 cup fresh squeezed lemon juice
1 or 2 TBS. honey
1/2 cup fresh dill chopped very fine
about 1 TBS. tamari
2 heaping TBS. good tasting nutritional yeast
1 heaping TBS. white miso
(must be white miso)
2 cloves garlic, smashed
1 TBS. dijon mustard

Combine all the ingredients in a blender and mix well.

TOFU MAYONNAISE
(or Sour Cream)
COMBINE IN A BLENDER:
1/2 block tofu
3 TBS. oil
juice of 1/2 lemon
salt and pepper to taste

Mix until smooth. Put in a bowl and stir in chopped pimentos if you like. Eggless!

DO YOU KNOW HOW TO TOAST NUTS???

The flavor of almost any nut is enhanced by toasting. Nuts may be toasted whole, chopped, or sliced. Use only enough to cover the bottom of a cast-iron skillet or cookie sheet. If you wish, toss them with a tablespoon each of oil and tamari (just enough to lightly cover). Place the pan in the oven or on the stove at a moderate heat and stir fairly often. Keep your eye on them; they'll be brown before you know it. The smell of roasting almonds is the best ever.

Another way is to spread nuts on a cookie sheet and roast in a pre-heated oven at 300^ to 325^ for about 20 minutes. If your nuts are in the shell, like peanuts, they keep cooking after you take them out of the oven. They may not need long.

HELL NO,
WE WON'T GLOW
SALAD DRESSING

3/4 cup olive oil or sesame oil
1/4 cup balsamic vinegar or lemon juice
1 level TBS. brown miso, mixed in 2 TBS. water
1 tsp. oregano
1 level TBS. tahini (optional)
dash of dry mustard

You know of course that miso gets rid of all kinds of pollutions in your body, not to mention radiation. Here is a great way to eat a little everyday.

Blend all the ingredients up in a blender and enjoy over a green salad or sliced tomatoes. This is also a good marinade for tofu or vegetables. For more about the super powers of miso see the Book of Miso, by William Shurleff and Akiko Aoyagi.

For a thicker dressing, add an avocado while everything is in the blender. Miso and avocado surprisingly lend themselves to each other.

EAST TENNESSEE FAVORITES

Greens

Aunt Sukie's Collard Greens

Fried Okra

Succotash

Great Smoky Mountain Green Beans

Black Eyed Peas And "Fat Back" Or "Hoppin' John"

"Fried Chicken" Tofu And Gravy

Josephina Fried Apples

Green Fried Tomatoes And Gravy

Tofu "Country Ham" And Red Eye Gravy

Okra A Go-Go

Old Time Corn Dodgers

Woodland Avenue Tomato Sandwiches

Tempest Side Spoon Bread

Flawless Corn Bread

Great Grandmother's Shortcake

Baking Powder Biscuits

Stickies

Three Sister's Pineapple Upside Down Cake

I LEAVE THIS RULE FOR OTHERS
WHEN I'M DEAD,
BE ALWAYS SURE YOU'RE RIGHT—
THEN GO AHEAD.
DAVY CROCKETT 1786-1836

GREENS

1 bunch collard greens
(or kale, chard, turnip greens, beet greens,
mustard greens; your favorite)
drop of oil (if your pan sticks)
dark sesame is best
touch of tamari mixed with 1/2 cup water
juice of a lemon, rice vinegar,
or hot pepper vinegar
salt and pepper to taste
cornbread on the side

Cut the stems off the greens and wash really good. You don't want them to be gritty. Put the greens on a table and cut them lengthwise a couple of times, then cut cross-wise in 1 inch strips. Add them to the pot with water they have retained on their leaves, plus about 1-2cups water with 1 TBS. tamari. Cover and cook over low heat about 45 minutes or until tender. Check water half way through ough cooking, add more if needed. Collards and mustard greens cook longer than kale or chard. The juice that is left over from this is called "potlikker" and is a true delicacy to the refined pallet.

Heap collards in a bowl and drizzle lemon or vinegar on top. Two or three pieces of corn bread are a must to use for sopping up the potlikker.

Aunt Sukie's Collard Greens

1 bunch collards or favorite greens,
left overs work the best
1 onion chopped up
2 TBS. dark sesame oil
1/2 to 1 cup dulce
-loosely packed and chopped up coarsely
1/2 block tofu
(strictly optional, if you're very hungry)
2 TBS. tamari
lemon juice or rice vinegar or Chinese black vinegar

Heat oil in a cast iron skillet. Add onions, tofu (cubed), and tamari. Saute until the onions are soft and the tofu is browned. Put in the dulce and let it all cook a few minutes. Add the cold greens, and barely toss, then cover. When heated through this is done.

Serve with corn bread or pones to dip in potlikker. Don't ask me why but this tastes just like it came out of Mammy's big fry pan. It is unbeatable.

P.S. If you never tasted country ham, the dulce reminds me of the intense saltiness of a piece of salt pork, so highly recommended by Southerners for cooking in a pot of greens.

Fried Okra

1 to 2 lbs. of okra
1/2 to 1 cup cornmeal
1/2 cup olive oil
1 to 2 tsp. garlic powder
1/2 tsp. salt and pepper

Rinse the okra and cut it in half lengthwise. Leave the ends on. Put the cornmeal, garlic powder, salt, and pepper into a paper bag, then add the okra and shake well. Heat the oil in a big skillet and add the okra. Don't heap the okra in the skillet, just make a couple batches. You want this to get crispy, not soggy. Don't stir this a lot, rather, turn it with a spatula. Drizzle a little tamari over it. When you eat these, pick them up at the nubby end, bite all the way down to the base, and discard the end, the way you would eat a shrimp. Left over boiled or steamed okra works fine too. Especially if you messed up and the okra got slimy.

SUCCOTASH

4 ears fresh corn
5 medium sized vine-ripened tomatoes
1/2 lb. okra or about 3 to 4 cups chopped up
bread crumbs (optional)
salt, pepper, and butter

There is no better summertime eating than succotash. Come end of July, first of August, corn gets to be twelve ears for a dollar. In the South you can't go two feet without someone offering you large bags of tomatoes from "the garden." If you are pressed for time and absolutely have to, you can substitute canned whole tomatoes in this recipe, but nothing can take the place of fresh corn and okra.

Cut corn off the cob and set aside. Skin tomatoes, chop up and add to corn. Cut ends off the okra and discard, then chop up the rest. Put okra pieces in a sauce pan barely covered in water and bring to a boil for about two minutes or so. Drain in colander. Combine okra in same bowl as corn and tomatoes and salt generously. Add pepper, pour into casserole dish, and dust with breadcrumbs if using. Then dot top generously with butter. Bake at 350 for one hour in deep dish, 45 minutes in a shallow one.

Some people put lima beans in their succotash; in East Tennessee we never did. This is a must have at a back yard picnic. Can be made the day before and kept in fridge till ready to be cooked.

GREAT SMOKY MOUNTAIN GREEN BEANS

**3 to 4 lbs. green beans, fresh
1/2 tsp. dry mustard
2 to 3 tsp. toasted sesame oil
about 2 garlic cloves
1 TBS. brown rice miso
1 onion chopped fine
lots of salt**

I will never forget the first time I had green beans after I left home. I was having dinner with my older cousin from New York. She put a big helping of beans on my plate and passed it over to me.

"Excuse me," I said, "my beans haven't been cooked yet." I handed my plate back to her.

"What do you mean, I just took them off the stove myself."

"Well, they are warm," I said, "but they're still crunchy."

"Of course they're crunchy," she said horrified, "you don't want to over cook them."

It was then that it dawned on me how the rest of the world eats green beans- what? cooked less than three hours? no ham bone? still crunchy? All good things come to an end. I've never had beans cooked exactly this way (not even in other parts of the South).

To string the beans, snip off the end with your finger and pull it down the length of the bean. Do this to both ends. Now you won't have any tough strings when you eat the beans.

Rinse the beans well and put into a large pot and cover with water. Bring to a boil and let cook a few minutes. Turn down the heat and simmer for about 7 hours or so. About halfway through cooking time, dip out some of the hot water into a cup and dissolve the miso into it. Add to the beans and let finish cooking. You can add the rest of the ingredients now too. As they finish cooking, the beans should be dark green. When you serve them, put several slices of tomato and raw onion on top, and slice into the beans. Eat all together. This is truly delicious. Don't worry about over cooking this; it can cook for 5 or 6 hours and keep getting better and better.

BLACK EYED PEAS AND "FAT BACK" OR "HOPPIN' JOHN"

2 or 3 cups black eyed peas washed and picked through
1 block of tofu (firm works best)
1/4 cup tamari mixed with 1/4 cup water
2 tsp. dry mustard
2 TBS. toasted sesame oil
1 or 2 cloves of garlic
1/2 tsp. savory
1 tsp. salt
2 tsp. ketchup, optional
2 tsp. Pick-a-Peppa Sauce
if you can't find this in your store, you may substitute worcestershire, A-1 Sauce, White Tiger Sauce, or Perkin's Steak Sauce, but Pick-a-Peppa works best...look for parrots on the label...there's another kind now too, Salsa Rica

I was brought up to believe that a pot of beans was simply not edible if it didn't have some type of meat cooked with it. I fiddled around until I came up with something that brings out the taste of the beans just like I remember.

Stir together the tamari, mustard, Pick-a-Peppa, garlic, and toasted sesame oil. Cut the tofu into nice sized chunks and toss gently with the marinade. The longer this soaks, the better it is, but if you don't have much time, about an hour should do it.

Put the beans in a pot with enough water to cover them, bring to a boil and add the onion, ketchup, and savory. Turn down and let simmer for about 45 minutes or so. When the peas are half done,

add the tofu and the rest of the marinade, salt, and pepper. Continue simmering and stir gently until the peas are soft. Serve this with hushpuppies or cornbread, collard greens, and boiled potatoes for good luck on New Year's Day.

"FRIED CHICKEN" TOFU AND GRAVY

My sister, Susan, made up this recipe. It is not only one of my favorites but I could eat it for breakfast, lunch, and dinner. I have never served this to anyone who did not love it, or say, "I can't believe it... this tastes just like fried chicken." It is really easy, and there are as many ways to make it as there are kitchens. Susan likes to let hers cook, covered, for a long time and get really juicy. I like mine crispy and greasy. I really encourage you to try this one.

HERE'S THE WAY I DO IT:
1 block tofu, sliced
2 to 3 TBS. sesame seeds
2 to 3 TBS. olive oil or as needed
2 TBS. tamari
1/2 cup good tasting nutritional yeast

Heat oil in skillet (electric skillet works best.) Add sesame seeds. While these are heating, take each slice of tofu and dredge in nutritional yeast until both sides are generously coated. When seeds start to sizzle, arrange tofu in skillet. Drizzle tamari over top. When crispy and brown, flip and fry other side till crispy. About 300 in electric skillet for about 30-45 minutes per side.

Gravy

1/4 to 1/3 stick margarine
big hand full flour
any left over nutritional yeast from tofu
1 or 2 cups soy milk, milk, or water
(milk makes a very thick and rich gravy, but
soy milk works just as well)
salt, pepper, and tamari

Leave the skillet just as it is from making the tofu, add the butter and let it melt. Stir in the flour and yeast until mixed and let brown a little but not burn. This should be done on medium-low heat. Add your liquid and continue stirring until thickened. Add salt, pepper and tamari.

Don't leave the drippings in your pan! Make gravy today! Enjoy over potatoes, rice, biscuits, stuffing, or whatever you're craving.

P.S. I also make this tofu in small cubes and have it in burritos or tortillas. It's great that way. It also tastes even better if it's left over. Try to make enough to put some back for the next day. This isn't easy though; however much I make, we always eat it all.

AUNT JOSEPHINA FRIED APPLES

8 to 10 thin skinned green apples
2 TBS. honey
1/4 to 1/2 cup maple syrup or brown sugar
1 to 2 TBS. brown rice miso
1 tsp. toasted sesame oil
butter or margarine

Cut the apples into quarters, or nice sized slices. Cut away the core and leave the peels on. Heat oil in a skillet over low heat. When it's hot, add the apples and stir around. While they are cooking, mix the maple syrup and miso into a paste and add to the apples. Usually about now I throw in about 1/2 stick of margarine just to be grandmotherly. Cover and cook over low heat for about an hour or so. Stir to keep from sticking when you have to.

I recently made this and used the juice of a lemon cause I thought it tasted good. It was so good I just had to add it to this recipe. Mix it in with the miso and syrup just like I said before. Everything else is the same. Oh yes, the sweetener, miso, and lemon can be altered to your individual taste; I normally leave the jar of syrup and the lemon by the stove and add as I lick the spoon.

Patsy says this tastes best eaten in big bites right from the skillet— or one bite at a time, snatched at weak moments straight from the fridge.

GREEN FRIED TOMATOES AND GRAVY

5 or 6 green tomatoes (these have to be hard and green, not even a little red)
1/2 cup cornmeal, preferably white
oil, as needed
salt and pepper

Heat some oil in a cast iron skillet. Slice the tomatoes and coat both sides with corn meal. Fry until tomatoes are soft inside and crispy outside, but not burnt. These tomatoes are good with real, down-home dinners of beans and potatoes, or for breakfast with tofu scrambled eggs, potatoes, and biscuits.

I almost forgot, be sure to make gravy with the tomatoes. When you have taken the last one from the pan, sprinkle in about 3 TBS. of flour and let it cook a few minutes until brown. Then stir in 1 or 2 cups of soy milk or milk, a touch of salt, and a bit of tamari or black coffee.
(Don't forget the grits!)

Tofu "Country Ham" AND Red Eye Gravy

1/4 cup tamari
3 to 5 TBS. sesame or olive oil
1 TBS. dijon mustard
1 big block of tofu
1 clove garlic, pressed

For this to work good you have to have "firm" tofu. If it seems too soft, let it sit in a colander to drain.

Pour about 1/4 cup tamari into a measuring cup, then fill about 1/2 full with water, add oil, mustard, garlic. At this point, depending on my mood, I stir in about 1 or 2 tsp. of any ONE of the following ingredients: horseradish, poppyseeds, chili powder, ginger, Pick-a-Peppa, ketchup, Old Bay Crab seasoning, you get the picture. Stir this together in a measuring cup. Cut tofu into cubes and spread in a glass pie plate. (You don't have to use a pie plate, it just works best for me... try to use something shallow and non-metallic.) Pour liquid over tofu and let sit 2 hours or as long as you can.

Heat a little oil in skillet and carefully add tofu with a slotted spoon (so grease won't spatter). When it's all in the skillet, add a little more of the marinade and let cook on medium until most of the liquid has cooked away and all sides are brown and crispy. Don't stir- rather scoot or turn with a spatula. This does not need a lot of standing over, best to just let it cook and turn occasionally.

When the tofu is well browned, remove from skillet and add rest of marinade. Let this come to a boil, and scrape any tofu off the bottom of skillet. Add one or two cups of strong, cold, black coffee, let return to a boil and remove from heat. That is red eye gravy. This is not a thick gravy but one that needs a biscuit to sop into it.

No, this is not exactly like country ham, but it is close— hot, greasy, and salty, YUM! This is excellent left over in a cold biscuit for a sack lunch.

Okra A Go-Go

1 or 2 lbs. fresh tender okra
How can you tell if okra is tender? If you can puncture the pod easily with your thumbnail, it's edible.

Quickly wash okra, leaving the ends on. Have salted boiling water ready. Add okra to water and let cook exactly 7 minutes after the water comes back to a boil. Not a minute more or less. Drain immediately and arrange in a circle around a bowl of your favorite dip or dressing. My favorite is blue cheese. Hot butter, lemon and garlic works well also.

Whether you're having dip or not, this is the best way to cook okra. If you like you can just pile on a serving plate, add a few pats of butter and dig in. Hold the okra by the tuff end and eat the tender part. It's a great finger food.

P.S. This method of cooking came from Marjorie K. Rawling's Cross Creek Cookery, the best cook book I have ever read.

OLD TIME CORN DODGERS

**2 1/4 cups white corn meal
(this should not be substituted... at home, we considered
yellow corn meal only good for feeding horses and pigs)
2 to 3 TBS. oil
(toasted sesame works really well)
about 1 cup buttermilk
(this can be diluted with 1/2 water)
1 1/2 tsp. baking powder
1 tsp. salt
1 TBS. honey only if you have used yellow corn meal**

Put the dry ingredients into a bowl and stir up. Make a well and add buttermilk and oil (honey if necessary) all at once. Stir up well; make it quick. Put big spoonfuls onto a hot, barely greased, low heat griddle. When brown on one side, turn over and let brown on the other; don't keep turning these back and forth. Keep a platter in a slow oven to keep the pones hot as they get done.

These are a must with vegetable soup, also collards, or any greens to sop up potlikker. With some butter and honey or jam, it'll cure a sweet tooth. This recipe has probably not changed a lick since a pioneer woman wrapped up a couple of pones and a few apples for her man to take to the field with him.

WOODLAND AVENUE TOMATO SANDWICHES

3 or 4 tomatoes
(if you can't pick these
from your backyard,
let the store bought ones
sit on your window sill
for a couple of days)
salt risen bread
mayonnaise
salt and pepper

The secret of this sandwich is that the bread must be sliced as thinly as possible. If you want, you can buy thin sliced bread, or just slice a piece in two. This may sound hard, but it's not really. I'll tell you the easiest way. First of all, use a good serrated bread knife. Also, fresh bread won't work, the best is a few days old. And lastly, bend down so that you are eye level with what you are doing. This makes all the difference in the world.

Okay... spread each piece of bread generously with mayo, and put 2 or 3 slices of tomatoes, depending on how big they are. Be sure to salt tomatoes now. Top the other piece of bread with mayo too. It's best to make a big plate of these cause you just can't stop eating them. They are perfect lunch or dinner in the hot dog days of August when tomatoes are coming in.

P.S. These sandwiches are great by themselves or sprinkled with a bit of good tasting nutritional yeast and toasted ground sesame seeds.

TEMPEST SIDE SPOON BREAD

1 cup soy milk or dairy milk
2 cups boiling water
1 cup white cornmeal must be white
1 tsp. salt
2 eggs or egg beaters
2 TBS. oil
2 tsp. baking powder

Spoon bread is about as old-timey good eatin' as you can get. I'm sure many pioneers served it as high falutin Sunday best. I best describe it as cornmeal souffle, which does no justice to the juicy, rich finished product. Most spoonbread makers have a few secrets, this is mine and it's unbeatable.

Put cornmeal, baking powder, in a bowl. Stir in oil. Let the water come to a boil, add salt and slowly stir the hot water into the cornmeal mixture. Do this slowly while stirring so the corn meal won't lump. If it does, use your whip on it.!!

Stir in milk, then oil and baking powder. Beat eggs in one at a time, and stir real good. Continue using whip. (Don't you just love the sound of that?!) I mean beat each egg long and hard.

Grease a deep casserole or souffle dish (remember, this will rise some). Bake in a pre-heated 400^ oven for about 40 or 45 minutes. This is done when it's puffed up and golden on top. Serve immediately with collards and/or black eyed peas. It should be served in the same dish it was cooked in. Be sure to take this to the table hot and you will be able to show off! This is also good for a girlfriend teaparty.

P.S. While this is cooking don't keep opening the oven door and peeking in, it will fall!

FLAWLESS CORNBREAD

What would we do without cornbread?? I make this at least twice a week and that's not enough. This is a dream of a recipe and can be used for corn muffins or corn sticks just as well as cooked in a skillet.

2 cups of cornmeal
(once again, white cornmeal)
1 tsp. salt
3 tsp. baking powder
1/3 cup flour
1 tsp. baking soda, if using buttermilk
3 to 4 TBS. corn oil
1 cup soy milk, sour soy milk, or buttermilk
1 egg or egg replacer
(I think it's just as good with no egg at all)

Pre-heat oven to 375^. Put one pat of butter or margarine in a cast iron skillet and put in oven. Mix dry ingredients in a bowl and make a well in it. Mix wet ingredients together and pour into the well. Stir well. Take hot skillet out of oven and tilt so butter runs all around edges. Pour batter into skillet and return to oven. Bake at 350^ for about 30 minutes. Take skillet out and run knife around edge. Turn upside down onto a serving plate or lift out with a spatula to plate. Serve hot with butter. Is there anything that doesn't go with cornbread?? Soup, vegetables, potatoes, beans, and with jam as a dessert. Is it possible to make collards or any greens for that matter and not make cornbread to go along with them? Summer or winter, dinner or breakfast, this recipe is a staple.

GREAT GRANDMOTHER'S SHORTCAKE

2 cups white or pastry flour
1 tsp. baking powder
pinch of salt
2 TBS. honey
1/2 cup margarine
1/2 cup milk (soy or dairy)

Sift the dry ingredients together and then work the margarine in with a fork. Add the milk and quickly stir with a fork until the dough leaves the side of the bowl. Roll the dough as thin as possible and cut out with a large cookie cutter. If you don't have one, you can use a wide mouth jar. Barely butter the top of a round and put another one on top of it. Do all of these little circles the same way, two high, and put on a greased cookie sheet. Then pop it into a 450^ oven. When they are brown, remove from the oven and separate immediately. These are glorious little things, not at all like you remember from the grocery store. I like to serve a big bowl of berries and a big bowl of these little shortcakes, so that my guests can stack them four high if they like (and they do).

Baking Powder Biscuits

2 cups flour (you can use whole wheat or unbleached white flour...
any combination of the two will also do fine...
just remember, the lighter the flour, the lighter the biscuit)
4 tsp. baking powder
1/2 tsp. salt
4 TBS. margarine
3/4 cups soy milk, milk, or water

There is something about making biscuits that gets me in touch with ancient ties of sisterhood with all women. Somehow, I feel a bond to pioneer ladies who made biscuits while they crossed the prairie; Okie mama's who whipped up batches of biscuits in Hooverville; big, black mammies who sent a platter of biscuits into the white folks, as well as down to the cabins.

Needless to say, I love biscuits. They are good for breakfast or supper and can be whipped up in no time. If you have any left over, these biscuits are the best for picnic or bag lunches. Try them split in half with soy-sage, "fried chicken" tofu, or just butter and jam.

Stir the dry ingredients together and work the margarine in with a fork until it's crumbly. Make a well and add the liquid all at once. Stir this quickly, just until the dough leaves the sides of the bowl. This shouldn't take more than 30 seconds. Turn this on to a well floured board and gently knead for about 30-40 seconds, just until you can roll out the dough without it sticking. Roll the dough to about 1/2 inch thick and cut with a biscuit cutter or cookie cutter. Even the end of a small glass will work. Put these on an ungreased cookie sheet and put in a hot oven, about 450^. Bake about 10 to 12 minutes, or until nice and brown on the bottom.

When cutting out biscuits, start in the center of rolled dough-this cuts waste. Cut straight down, don't twist.

Stickies

My first real encounter with "stealth" must have been at one of Granny's backyard picnics, the 4th of July probably. It was always a big turnout with lots of aunts, uncles, and cousins. Shorty did the steaks on the grill, the grown-ups all played croquet, and Granny basically just ran around counting and recounting people to make sure she had enough plates, glasses, knives, napkins, and such put out.

Us kids were left to run wild, which consisted mainly of fighting over the hammock until someone finally got hurt and we weren't allowed to play there anymore or playing in the old Studebaker parked in the garage. It hadn't been started in at least ten years or so, but it still had it's place lined up with the rest of the cars (it had the most wonderful old, earthen leather smell).

My favorite game was sneaking up the back steps to sneak a stickie. When the tables were all set and it seemed like Granny might possibly have come up with a total, that meant it was safe to start up the steps. Now, you have to understand, this was a long, creaky, wooden staircase in full view of the whole backyard, flower garden, croquet court, grill and all. The added danger was the fact that two years earlier we'd eaten all the stickies before dinner and weren't even allowed to go Near That Kitchen. We were being educated in the fine art of stealth and motivated by the powder of sugar (a double whammy if there ever was one). Not just sugar but Granny Sugar. When we finally made it to the kitchen it was like we had died and gone to Candy Land. There were brownies, blackberry pie, praline cookies, cheese cake (we called it white pie), red velvet cake, and stickies.

It took a few minutes just to let your eyes feast on all that food and to figure out which stickie you could take without the plate looking cockeyed. I got to be very sneaky at this. Mama was always walking silently in on me, causing my heart to practically stop beating and forcing me to drop my stickie in mid-air. You could normally hear Granny coming as she was usually talking to herself, "Bettie and Bernie, that makes 19 and 20, Susan and Bill, 21, 22..."

It was like those stickies had some kind of voodoo spell on me. I just couldn't stay away. I have made these many times since but like Granny's creamed corn, it just cannot be duplicated. I think it has a lot to do with her kitchen.
Stickies are usually made up of the bits of dough left over after you've made a pie. If you haven't made a pie and want to have a little sweet pastry anyway, here's how:

2 cups flour
1/2 to 1/4 cup brown sugar
1 tsp. salt
cinnamon
4 to 5 tsp. ice water
a little less than 1/2 cup margarine

Mix and roll out like you would a pie crust (if you don't know how, read something about it in the chapter on pies). Sprinkle brown sugar over the top. You can use honey or maple syrup but it will be messier, and even stickier if that's possible. Dot with margarine and sprinkle with a dash of cinnamon. Roll up into a thick roll like a cigar. Then slice the roll into 1/4 to 1/2 inch pieces. Place these close together on a cookie sheet, so they wont come apart. Bake in a slow oven, about 325^ for about 30 minutes. Take these out of the pan while they are still warm or they will stick badly.

THREE SISTER'S PINEAPPLE UPSIDE DOWN CAKE

4 TBS. margarine or butter
1/2 to 1 cup of your favorite sweetener
(I have used just about all of them successfully— honey, brown sugar, maple sugar, even molasses, but this is one of the few recipes that I do use brown sugar mixed with honey)
4 to 5 slices of pineapple, fresh or canned
1/2 cup whole pecans

This is the mixture that you put into the skillet first. Melt the butter and the sweetener together in the bottom of a cast iron skillet, very slowly. When this has melted, arrange the pineapple and pecans in the skillet, too, and be sure to make this look good, as it will be the top of the finished cake. Now here is the batter:

1/4 cup margarine
1/2 cup plus 2 TBS. sweetener
1 egg or egg replacer
1 1/2 cup unbleached white flour
(whole wheat will do also)
2 1/2 tsp. baking powder
1/2 tsp. salt
1/4 cup evaporated milk mixed with 1/4 cup water, or if you used can pineapple, use the juice left in the can
1/2 tsp. vanilla

Cream the margarine and the honey (if there is a man around, bat your eyelashes and ask him to do it for you). Then add the egg (you can do this while he's stirring). Stir the dry ingredients togeth-er and add alternately with the milk mixture. Stir in the vanilla. Pour batter carefully over fruit in skillet and bake at 350^ for about 45 minutes or until done.

A note about taking it out of the pan: Get a good, dependable potholder and the plate you're going to be serving the cake on. Use one of your best plates because after you see how wonderful it looks, you'll wish you had. First, run a knife around the edge of the skillet to separate it from the cake. Now, place the dish directly on top of it, face down. Grip the handle of the skillet. With one hand on the plate, flip the whole thing over in one big motion. The skillet should come right off. Do this in front of someone and they will be wildly impressed.

VEGETABLES AND CASSEROLES

Wok Of Ages

Hash Browns

Matilda's Summer Squash

Onion Shortcake

Granny's Famous Creamed Corn

Mexican Beans

Fresh Corn Fritters

Baba Ganoush

Hummus

Milwaukee Street Squash

Posh

How To Bake Squash

CAULIFLOWER IS NOTHING
BUT CABBAGE WITH
A COLLEGE EDUCATION.
MARK TWAIN 1835-1910

IT WAS AS TRUE...
AS TURNIPS IS.
IT WAS AS TRUE...
AS TAXES IS.
AND NOTHING'S TRUER
THAN THEM.
CHARLES DICKENS 1812-1870

WOK OF AGES

I use my wok so much sometimes, I feel like it must be suffering from an identity crisis. It is the greatest for making popcorn. Sometimes I make gravy in it, and in a pinch I've used it for tomato sauce. I love to make vegetables in a wok; they get so sweet. Here's a basic recipe and the way I do it:

2 onions, sliced in crescents
2 carrots, sliced diagonally
2 or 3 stalks broccoli
about 1 TBS. oil
1 or 2 TBS. tamari
generous grating of ginger

Put the wok over medium to high flame and add oil. In a well seasoned wok you won't need much, just brush the bottom with a pastry brush. When it's good and hot, add the onions. I almost always start off my wok vegies with onion or garlic, or both. Stir these until they are just coated with oil.

At this point, forget everything you've ever heard about cooking in a wok. You're not really stirring, but sort of tossing with two wooden paddles. There is an old saying, "too much care spoils the child." I don't know about real life, but in cooking, this rule holds true. The food will cook okay all by itself; stirring it around too much will just make it mushy. If you really love to stir, make a lot of gravy, or quick stir fried vegetables.

When the onions are half done, add the sliced carrots, toss and drizzle a little tamari over the top. After it cooks about 5 minutes, add the chopped broccoli and a generous grating of ginger over the top. Toss a little and cover. Let cook about 5 more minutes. The broccoli will turn bright green-that means it's almost done but still crunchy. Give

it a few more minutes and stir a few more times. The onions should be brown and roasted by now.

Of course, there are a million different combinations; this is just the basic way of doing it. I try not to use more than 3 or 4 ingredients at once. If you use too many, they all sort of get lost in each other. Enjoy!

HERE'S HOW TO MAKE HASH

HASH BROWNS

Why do hash browns always taste best at some greasy spoon 100 miles from nowhere? Some meals are not complete with out a side of potatoes. Come to think of it, I make whole meals of just fried potatoes.

THIS IS THE WAY I DO IT. YOU'LL NEED:

About 4 to 6 medium to large potatoes... leftover boiled or baked potatoes work well here
1/2 to 1 onion chopped up small
1 clove garlic, smashed and chopped
olive oil
plenty of salt and pepper

Boil the potatoes whole and let cool (at least enough to handle). If I am ever making potatoes for anything, I make a lot because I know I can use any leftovers for hash browns. Chop into cubes, then cover bottom of cast iron skillet with oil. Heat oil and add chopped onion. Let cook a few minutes then add potatoes. This is a secret: don't pile too many potatoes in the skillet, just make two pans at once; they will taste better. Salt and pepper generously and cook over medium heat. Turn with a spatula after cooking 5 minutes or so. The bottoms should be brown and crispy. Let the other side cook until they are done the way you like them. Drizzle on a little more oil or butter if you need to.

For a fancier dish, add a few chopped mushrooms and 1/2 a green pepper, chopped, when adding the onion. I almost forgot, a little sage or paprika sprinkled over the top when cooking is really yummy.

MATILDA'S SUMMER SQUASH

4 yellow summer squash
about 2 red or onions
3 or 4 big, red, ripe-from-the-backyard tomatoes (if you can't get these and have to settle on supermarket tomatoes, let them sit in the window for a couple of days to ripen up a bit)
a few dots of butter
1 tsp. basil
salt

This is my favorite vegetable recipe. The colors are wonderful, and the onions get so sweet you won't believe it.

Slice all three vegetables into thin rounds and layer into a casserole dish (a long thin one will work best). Put a fine sprinkle of basil and salt on the tomato layer. Dot the squash layer with butter. If you ever eat parmesan cheese, now is the time. Just sprinkle some on when you do the margarine. Continue layering until the ingredients are used up. Make the last layer one of bread crumbs and dots of butter. Bake this in a pre-heated 350^ oven for about an hour or until the squash is tender. You can pile this up a little bit, when you're layering it as the tomatoes and squash will shrink considerably.

Onion Shortcake

2 cup whole wheat flour
4 tsp. baking powder
1/2 tsp. salt
4 TBS. oil or margarine
1/2 to 2/3 cup soy milk

3 TBS. margarine
3 TBS. flour (chick pea, rice, or whole wheat)
1 cup soy milk or water
1 TBS. miso dissolved into the liquid

4 or 5 onions

The first thing you are going to do is cook the onions so they can be cooling while you are doing everything else. Saute the onions in a little oil and when they are soft, set them aside till you are ready for them.

Now, you are going to make a biscuit out of the first 5 ingredients. If you've never made biscuits, check out the recipe for baking powder biscuits. Mix the dry ingredients, and cut in the oil or margarine with 2 knives. Add the soy milk and stir a little. Turn out and knead a few times. Press this into a greased casserole dish. Spread the cooled onions over the dough. Next, comes a miso sauce and again, if you've never made a sauce, read a bit in the chapter on sauces. Melt margarine in the same pan used to cook the onions. Add flour and make a paste. Remember to dissolve the miso in the liquid and when that's done, add it to the paste. Stir it around and when it's done, remove

from heat. You can add a touch of tamari if you have it. Pour this over the onions and bake in a 400^ oven for about 15 to 20 minutes or until the dough is done.

This is a good dish to have instead of mashed potatoes and gravy or biscuits and gravy.

GRANNY'S FAMOUS CREAMED CORN

5 or 6 cups of corn, scored and to score run knife thru kernels before cutting off the cob
3 TBS. margarine or butter
2 TBS. honey or sugar
1/4 to 1/3 cup flour
1/2 cup soy or dairy milk
1/2 tsp. salt
black pepper

Cut the corn off the cob into a bowl (you don't want to waste any of the juice). Melt the margarine in a pan and stir in the flour, then honey. Let this cook a few minutes and then add the corn with it's juice. Give it a stir and add the liquid, salt, and pepper. Stir this occasionally. It shouldn't take long to thicken. Put a few dots of butter on top and serve immediately. When I go to Granny's for dinner, she makes a huge bowl of creamed corn and puts it right on my plate... isn't it nice to be indulged?

P.S. I think one of Granny's secrets is that she always uses sweet white corn like Silver Queen. She gets lots in the summer, cuts it off the cob, and freezes it. We enjoy creamed corn all winter long.

MEXICAN BEANS

1 to 3 cups of dry beans, pintos or bolita are good...It's nice to throw in a handful of red beans also. Remember, beans triple in size so don't cook too many.

4 to 6 cups of water or as needed

1/4 cup oil

2 to 3 tsp. savory (this is especially good in Mexican beans... I usually put a dash in most beans that I make because it's supposed to not make you fart as much)

2 to 3 tsp. cumin

1 tsp. cayenne

2 to 3 tsp. oregano

2 onions, chopped

2 cloves garlic

couple dashes tabasco

salt

Soak the beans over night. Rinse them off well and put in a deep pot, covered generously with water. Add every-thing except the salt and onions. Let it come to a boil and stay there a few minutes. Cover, turn down, and let simmer about 2 hours. Stir these every so often and add more water when you need to. When the beans feel soft, add the onions and salt and let them finish cooking uncovered. This will push the gas out of the beans now, so it won't end up in you later.

If you have 1/2 a jar of tomato juice sitting around, pour that in. Or if you have a few ripe tomatoes sitting in the window, chop them up and throw 'em in. Run some water in the bottom of a ketchup bottle, swish it around, and pour that in too. If you don't have any of these things, no problem; your beans will still be good.

Let the beans cook another hour or so until they get really juicy. Don't forget to add more water if you have too. Cover and let sit until dinner time. I like the beans just like this. Some people I know though, like to put them in the blender and make a nice taco filling.

These beans are great in burritos, enchiladas, que-sadillas, or a side dish to any Mexican meal. Don't stop there though; sopping up the juice of the beans with a piece of corn bread or hushpuppy is what it's all about.

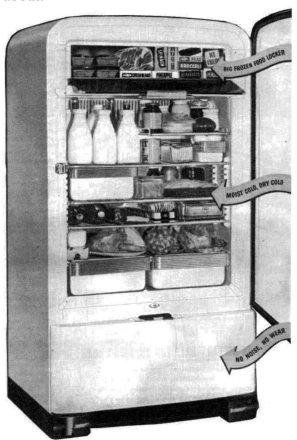

Fresh Corn Fritters

1 cup flour
1 cup liquid(water, milk, beer, mineral water)
1 tsp. baking powder
touch of honey
1/4 cup oil
2 eggs or egg replacers
1/2 onion chopped fine (optional)
salt and pepper
1 1/2 to 2 cups corn, or chopped kale, spinach,
grated carrots, zucchini, left-over noodles,
mashed potatoes, onions, etc.

Mix all the ingredients in a bowl. Mix it up good
so there are no lumps. Stir in the vegetables last.
Get your skillet good and hot. Don't turn it up as
high as it will go because this causes the outside to
brown while the inside stays doughy. This is a thin
batter; I like mine that way. Put a little oil or margarine in the skillet. You don't want to fry these;
you want just enough oil so the fritter won't stick.
Pour in some batter with a tablespoon. I usually
scoot the edges of the fritter back with a spatula,
so I can get 2 or 3 in the skillet at the same time.
If you are making a lot, use 2 skillets, as it will go
twice as fast. These cook just like pancakes; when
the top is covered with little air holes, turn them
over and let them brown on the other side. The
last ones always come out best.

I have never been much of a pancake eater, but I
can eat corn fritters by the 1/2 dozen. This is
another one of those recipes that sound too easy
to be good; trust me...don't worry if the first few
stick and tear up. You usually have to sacrifice a
few to the great fritter god in the sky.

BABA GANOUSH
OR
BABA GANOOJI
OR
I THINK SENTER'S FAINTED

This is a very authentic recipe. Patsy used to make
this at a little middle eastern restaurant, and that's
who taught me to make it. She said the smell of
eighty burned eggplants every morning was pretty
intense, but you'll just be using two or three. This
may sound a little strange, but it's a very easy
recipe and tastes like something I can't compare to
anything (although once someone told me it tasted
like dirty socks). I love baba ganoush, and my
brother Senter, well, the title describes his reaction.

2 to 3 medium egg plants
1/4 to 1/2 cup tahini
juice of 1 lemon (large)
1/2 tsp. salt
1 clove garlic, smashed and chopped

This is easiest done over a flame, either from your gas stove or the grill. Lay an egg plant directly over your gas burner. Trust me, just lay it over and turn it on; it's supposed to burn. If you don't have a gas stove, put it in a pan right under the broiler. This is easiest on an outside grill. Make sure it burns on all sides. Don't get freaked out and think you've done something wrong and take it off the stove before it is really good and burnt all over. I know it will be dripping and steaming- it cleans right up.

So, when it is charred, take it to the sink and peel all the burned skin off. It's okay to run water over it. When you are done you should have a nice piece of roasted eggplant. Sort of smash this up with your hands in a bowl and add the other ingredients. This is to your own taste. If you are using 3 big eggplants you'll want to use 1/2 cup of tahini and maybe a whole lemon instead of a half. Just add them a little at a time and taste as you go. When done, spread on a nice serving platter, crumble a few pinches of oregano over the top, and drizzle about 1 TBS. olive oil over the whole thing.

Let chill and serve with pita bread and vegetables. This is a must side-dish for any middle eastern dinner. It has a smokey flavor that comes from the burning. I tried it once in a skillet and it just wasn't as good though.
P.S. Sometimes the eggplant might be a little stringy. If so, put it in the processor for a few seconds. You don't want it smooth, but not real lumpy and stringy either.

HUMMUS

This is another recipe Patsy learned at a middle eastern restaurant. It's very easy and very good. We like it with pita bread and vegetables but it also makes super sandwiches. Hummus is a lot more Americanized than Baba Ganoush, yet it still has something ancient about it.

3 to 4 cups cooked chick-peas (about 1 cup dry) (save some of the water they cooked in)
1/3 to 1/2 cup tahini
juice of 1 or 2 lemons
3/4 tsp. salt
1 to 2 cloves garlic, smashed and minced
pinch of paprika
pinch of oregano
1 TBS. olive oil

Put the chick-peas in the food processor with enough of the water to blend into a very smooth paste. You don't want this to be runny at all, just a smooth, thick paste. Just add the water a little at a time until it is the consistency you want. Add the tahini, lemon, garlic, and salt and keep blending. When well mixed, taste and adjust. No ingredient should be dominating the others.

Spread on a nice platter. Wave the back of a knife through it. Crush and sprinkle on the oregano, then paprika, and drizzle oil over the top. Let chill for one hour.

Milwaukee Street Squash

2 yellow onions
1 butternut, acorn, haikido, pumpkin, or any
winter squash
toasted sesame oil
1/2 to 1 cup cooked hiziki(optional)
touch tamari

This recipe is a credit to the phrase "give me the simple life." It is easy, and the taste is truly unbeatable. The onions and squash get sweeter and sweeter as they cook. Don't feel you have to put the seaweed in, but why not?? Even devout seaweed haters have loved this at my house. This is something that really hits the spot when you are hungry for real food.

Do this in a wok or deep cast iron pot or an electric skillet. Pour in the oil and let it start to get hot. Slice the onions into thin crescents and add to oil. Toss barely and go to the squash. Cut in half and scoop out the seeds and pulp. Lay flat side down and cut slices as thin as possible. When the onions are transparent add the squash all at once. Toss barely again, making sure the flame is low. Drizzle a little tamari over the top and add a little more oil if it is starting to stick. Don't cover this, it takes awhile for it to cook. The squash should be very soft and almost roasted. If you are using seaweed, wakame, arame, and hiziki are all good. Just cook (let soak in cold water for about one hour or barely simmer for about 20 minutes) first and add to the squash during the second half of the cooking time.

P.S. This should cook slowly and stay juicy; if it starts to stick and you don't want to use more oil, dilute a little tamari in water and pour over top (no more than about 1/4 cup of liquid though).

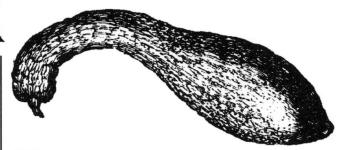

POSH

One night my friend threw a big party and everyone happened to bring a few friends, an unexpected cousin from out of town or someone they happened to meet on the bus on the way over. It was a dinner party and by the time half of the people had arrived, Cathy knew that there wasn't going to be enough food. This is what she came up with and ever since it's been one of my favorites.

4 or 5 potatoes
1/2 to 1 winter squash (any kind)
salt, pepper, and margarine

Cut up the potatoes and squash (scoop seeds out of squash) and boil together until soft. Leave peels on potatoes if you want and scoop out squash from its skin. Mash with potato masher or put in a mixer until smooth. Add salt and pepper and lots of butter or margarine. Keep in a warm oven till ready to serve.

HOW TO BAKE A SQUASH
Cut the squash in half and lay flat side down in a baking dish in about 1/4 inch of water. Bake 30 minutes at 350 then turn over and drop a pat of butter into the cup. Bake 30 more minutes at the same temperature. This works perfectly and keeps squash from drying out.

42

GRAINS

IT WAS STRANGE TO FEEL
SO PURE A JOY IN THE SIMPLE
TASK OF PREPARING A
BREAKFAST. THE WORK
SEEMED AN END TO ITSELF,
AS IF THE MOTIONS OF FILLING
A COFFEE POT, SQUEEZING
ORANGES, SLICING BREAD
WERE PERFORMED FOR THEIR
OWN SAKE, FOR THE SORT OF
PLEASURE ONE EXPECTS,
BUT SELDOM FINDS, IN THE
MOTIONS OF DANCING.

AYN RAND

HOW TO MAKE
BROWN RICE

I was lucky. I learned to make rice from an old Spanish lady in Puerto Rico. She lived in a slummy housing project and had a little stand where she made rice and beans at lunch time. She sold it to the people there, in the project or to whoever was hanging out on the corner that day. Until I met this lady, I had never enjoyed a bowl of real rice in my life. It was always soupy or sticky, you all know, a lumpy mass of something served with mushy vegetables and spiritual overtones.

What a cook this lady was. Her menu never varied from rice and beans, but I never tasted the same thing twice and I ate there every day. She couldn't speak a word of English and my Spanish was horrible but I learned. They should try cooking at the U.N. sometime instead of talking.

Start with a good sized pot, or any pot with a tight fitting lid. If you don't have anything else, use a dinner plate to cover the pan. Put a little oil in the pan and let it get hot. Bring the rice back to life by rinsing it under cold water in a strainer, then add the rice to the hot oil. Stir around to coat rice and let it roast a few minutes. If you are planning to add any herb, spice, chopped onion, or pepper, do it now and let it all cook together a few minutes.

Now it's time to add water. If you like dry rice, add 1 3/4 cups of water for every cup of rice. For moister rice, add 2 to 2 1/4 cups water for 1 cup rice. Go ahead now and add salt and pepper and a touch of tamari. Don't stir this again. It's very important to remember, don't stir this! Okay, let the rice come to a boil and cook about 5 minutes like that, then cover and turn flame or burner to very low and let simmer for 45 minutes. Remember (and this is the big secret), after you put the lid on the rice, don't lift it again. Don't even think about going near the lid. If you do it just like this you'll be guaranteed perfect rice. If you have a layer of brown crusty rice on the bottom of the pan, scrape it off and eat it yourself—it's the best part of the rice.

As I read over this recipe I realize I have not emphasized enough the fact that you absolutely, positively, cannot lift up the lid after you have put it on the rice. Not even for a minute, not even for a second. The first two weeks I worked with my lady friend, every time my hand went near the pot, she would cock back her spoon ready to give me a good wack if I so much as touched it. So remember, and let the people in your house know, that when they come in and say, "Wow, what smells so good???" and get ready to lift the lid and sniff, you are going to be standing guard with your spoon cocked and ready.

GARLIC GRITS

It was a hard day in the hills and her back hurt like hell. Roping cows was something she always hated doing, roping cows or laying in the sun. Laying in the shade, now that's a horse of a different color.

She could see the house from where she was on the ridge. Good, the lights were on, maybe the coffee was started.

On her way from the barn to the house, Delores picked up a couple of good sized logs. "How could I be ready for a fire," she wondered, "I got so darned hot today I thought I was going to keel over." She made her way up the porch steps and let the door slam behind her. "Yeah, it's me," she answered, "God, my dogs is beat!" About that time, she rounded the corner from the hall into the kitchen and knew that the worst part was over. Coffee was made, the rocker was empty, and Patsy had on her blue apron.

Patsy was leaned over the table cutting out biscuits. "I had some sour milk so I figured I'd use it up in these." As she said this, she turned to face Delores, the first time since she'd come home. Her eyes were the prettiest things Delores had seen all day. Patsy wiped her hands on her apron. "What you need, you poor little thing?"

"Some grits?," said Delores hopefully.

"They're already on."

1 cup grits
4 1/2 cups water
1/2 tsp. salt
1 stick margarine
1 egg or egg replacer
3/4 cup milk or soy milk
2 cloves garlic
3/4 to 1 cup sharp cheddar cheese (grated)
or 1 cup soy/yeast cheese or soy cheese

Cook the grits in salted water until mushy. Do this over low heat. Stir in margarine, egg, and milk. Next, stir in the garlic, smashed and chopped, cheese and whatever else you want to add. Obviously, you have to stir this up quite a lot. Pour into a greased baking dish, and bake 35 minutes at 350^.

JUST PLAIN GRITS

Follow the directions according to the package. These are pretty hard to mess up. They need lots of butter, and you can go from there. Good tasting nutritional yeast is great, parmesan is also, as is chopped umeboshi plumb, hot sauce, toasted nuts of any kind, and even gravy. Grits are served on a plate, not a bowl. When left over, you'll find they congeal into a cold lump. Put this in the fridge and when ready to use again, slice them up and fry them. Yum. If you can't find grits at your grocery store, the next time you are traveling in the south, you can get a five pound bag which ought to do you for a bout a year.

Basmati Rice

2 cups basmati rice (there is a new kind now grown in Texas that's just as good... it cooks the same and is called Texamati)
3 cups water
pat of margarine
pinch of salt

This is a wonderful rice. It is one of my favorite grains and I can eat big bowls full. It is a very light grain, like cous-cous, and is very good in the summer when it's too hot to cook much or work up an appetite for something heavy. It is also good to have with any intensely spicy side dish. I like it with chutney, barbecue sauce, chili, and mexican food. It is also a good rice to use in casseroles because it can absorb a lot of moisture and still be light without becoming sticky or lumpy. This kind of rice also makes great fried rice. Here's how to make it:

The ratio of water to rice is 1 1/2 parts water to 1 part rice. Remember, basmati can soak up a lot of water, so if you put in a little too much by mistake it won't hurt.

Put the water in a pot (with a tight fitting lid) and bring to a boil. Add margarine and salt and rice. Sometimes basmati can be real dirty, so you should rinse it real well with cold water first in a strainer. Let the rice continue to boil for a few minutes and then turn it down to low and cover. Let this cook unstirred and absolutely undisturbed for 30 minutes.

This is ready to serve now, but if you're not ready yet, toss it very gently, replace the lid, and let continue to steam until you're ready.

COUS★COUS

1 cup cous-cous per 1 1/2 cup water
any 1 or 2 vegetables— yellow or green onion,
mushrooms, green peppers, carrots, bok choy,
corn cut off cob, etc. (traditional vegetables are
chick peas, carrots, turnips, zucchini cut into
strips, and raisins)
couple pats of butter or margarine

Cous-cous is the summer time grain; you can have a "hot meal" without heating up your kitchen. It's ready in just ten minutes. Really.

Saute vegetables until about half done. Add water and butter and cover. When it comes to a boil stir in cous-cous and as it returns to a boil re-cover and turn off the burner. It's ready in about 10 minutes or whenever water is absorbed.

FIRST DATE MILLET AND ONIONS

I had been asked out on a dinner date. I was excited, expecting candles, music, wine, or at least one of the above. Instead, I got a big kind of glucky pot of millet and onions. That was it, no serving dish, no salad, no vegetable, no bread, no chocolate. I don't even think there was any butter. But hey, I have an open mind and I was starving. Anyway, it was delicious, and it just goes to show that if something is made with positive vibes, good things come out of it. I learned something about millet that night and the guy and I, we got married!

1 cup millet
1 3/4 to 2 cups water
2 carrots or one onion chopped in matchsticks
(millet tends to get a little lumpy if
cooked by itself... mix it with your
favorite vegetable... I like carrots)
1 TBS. sesame oil
tamari
salt and pepper

Heat oil in pot, add carrots or onions and let cook for a few minutes. Rinse off millet in cold water and add to cooking vegetables. Let millet roast a few minutes. Add salt, pepper, and tamari, a dash of each, a little more salt, then the water. Let come to a boil then cover and let simmer about 30 to 40 minutes.

This sounds plain, but it hits the spot. It's worth a try on a cold winter night. If you make this with carrots, grill some onions to serve over it. It's really a great dish.

❧BASIC❧
CORNBREAD
DRESSING

I call this basic dressing because no two dressings ever come out the same. You may want to add a little left- over rice, omit the carrots and add more nuts; do what you like, this is a good recipe to experiment with. It's deceptively simple, and also the best way ever to use your left over corn bread. Take note—when they made stuffing at my great grandmother Hunter's house she could be heard to call out more than once, "Don't stir the dressing, it'll clump!"

1/4 to 1/2 pan of left over corn bread (this can't be "Yankee" cornbread made with honey or sugar, that tastes like cake)
2 cloves garlic, mashed and chopped
2 or 3 celery stalks, sliced and chopped
1 or 2 onions, diced
2 or 3 carrots cut into match sticks
1/2 to 1 cup roasted pecans, walnuts, chestnuts, sunflower seeds, or any of your favorite nuts (be sure they're roasted)
butter and olive oil (sesame oil can be substituted for olive if you want)
1/2 bunch of parsley, chopped
salt and lots of black pepper
1/4 cup water mixed with 1/4 cup tamari
several large pats of butter

YOU MAY WANT TO EXPERIMENT WITH THESE HERBS:
    1 TBS. sage, very loose
    1/4 tsp. rosemary
    1/2 tsp. thyme

Heat oil in skillet, electric skillet works best, add garlic, onions, carrots, herbs, and celery, in that order. Let cook about medium for about 10 minutes or so. The vegetables should be rendering a little juice. If not, or if the mixture has started to stick at any time, add the tamari water. Cover and let cook about 5 more minutes. By this time, it should be very juicy on the bottom. Crumble cornbread finely right into the pan. Since this is left over it'll be dry and will crumble easily. Make sure it is crumbs, hunks aren't good. If you have any left over rice you can add this now also. Barely toss this, add parsley, big pats of butter, and chopped, roasted nuts. Turn heat to very low, cover and let steam about 15 minutes or so.

For a nice change, omit any vegetable and add soy-sage. Or omit cornbread and add wild rice. Or omit carrots and add mushrooms.

Remember though, don't stir this, rather toss gently with a spatula. If you don't use an electric skillet use a heat diffuser toward the end.

Don't wait until Thanksgiving or Christmas to have stuffing. The ingredients are usually just sitting around in your refrigerator. This dressing really is the supreme.

Johnny Reb Dirty Rice

This is real traditional, down-home Southern cookin' at its best. Dirty rice is originally made with chicken livers; here's how I do it. It's an easy recipe and a great change from plain rice.

4 to 5 cups cooked rice (left over will do fine)
1 red onion, chopped
1 bunch green onions, chopped
1 green pepper, chopped
2 cloves garlic, smashed and chopped
1/2 teaspoon cayenne pepper
1/2 cup parsley, chopped
1 cup broken pecans, peanuts, or walnuts

SAUCE:
1/4 cup tamari
2 tsp. dry mustard
2 TBS. dark sesame oil
1 TBS. prepared horse radish
1 TBS. basalmic vinegar

Saute onions, garlic, and green pepper until soft. Add nuts and red pepper and continue cooking. Put tamari in measuring cup and add water to make about 1/2 cup. Add other sauce ingredients, stir well and add to skillet mixture. Turn down heat and cover.

Grease a rectangular casserole dish. Add parsley to skillet mixture and then recover. Spread rice in bottom of casserole, and spread skillet mixture over it. Dot generously with butter. Bake at 350^ for 20 minutes, or about 30 minutes if cold rice is used.

This is a great dish to have with tofu or tempeh, baked squash, or sweet potatoes.

Kasha With Home Fries
OR
Annie Hall Goes to Russia

2 onions, chopped
2 or 3 potatoes, sliced or chopped
2 cups kasha buckwheat
3 1/2 cups boiling water
1 TBS. tamari
1 tsp. thyme
1/2 to 1 cup sliced mushrooms
salt and pepper
oil, as needed

Saute the onion, mushrooms, and potatoes until the onions are translucent and the potatoes are 1/2 done. Add the buckwheat and toss until evenly distributed. Add boiling water, salt, pepper, tamari, and thyme. Cover and simmer about 30 minutes.

For me, Kasha by itself is just too heavy. I like to cook it with a couple of other vegetables. Carrots and celery work good. Gravy is real good on buckwheat too. Serve this on a snowy night with onion shortcake and baked squash.

POPCORN

No, I'm not kidding. Popcorn is one of my main staples. I feel like people forget popcorn until it's movie time. I would rather have popcorn than any other food. Here are the things I like on my corn, and all the many ways I've cooked it.

№1 Good tasting nutritional yeast. This is a must; if you haven't had yeast on your corn you haven't lived.

№2 Pop it with a little garlic or onion salt or a pinch of oregano or basil.

№3 Kelp, paprika, and sesame salt are also good on popcorn.

№4 Store your corn in an air tight jar. Some people say keep your corn in the refrigerator or freezer. I do this but don't really know if it does anything or not.

№5 A wok works great for popping corn.

№6 A touch of olive or toasted sesame oil is good in with the other oil used for popping.

№7 Drizzle a little tamari on top instead of melted butter for a change.

№8 Popcorn is the perfect traveling food. Make a bag full before a long trip.

№9 Spike or Vegie-Salt is good on popcorn.

№10 A big bowl of popcorn and a Greek salad is my favorite summertime dinner.

CAJUN RED BEANS AND RICE

1 lb. red beans or red kidney beans
1 bunch chopped green onions (including the tops)
2 or 3 bermuda onions, chopped
2 cloves garlic, smashed and chopped
1 bunch parsley, chopped
several sticks of celery(including the leaves)
1/2 tsp. cayenne
6-8 cups steamed hot rice
salt to taste, added after beans are soft

Let the beans soak over night.

Saute the onions, garlic, and half of the scallions. Rinse the beans and add to onions, stir around and add about 6 cups of water and the celery. Let come to a boil, then turn down and let simmer about 2 hours. Check it every once and a while and add water if necessary. Towards the end of cooking time stir and mash the softest beans against the edge of the pot to sort of thicken it all up. Add the salt.

Serve the beans with a big bowl of rice and a bowl of the chopped green scallions.

P.S. If you would like, you can make tofu fat-back and add it to these beans the last 30 minutes or so of cooking time.

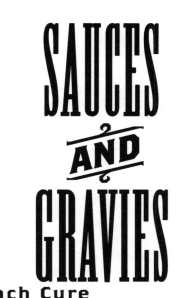

SAUCES AND GRAVIES

GOD BLESS MAMA AND DADDY;
AND RICE AND GRAVY.
PRAYER OF AN ANONYMOUS CHILD

ALL I WANT TO
MAKE ME HAPPY;
TWO LITTLE BOYS
TO CALL ME PAPPY.
ONE NAMED SOP,
ONE NAMED GRAVY;
ONE FOR THE ARMY,
ONE FOR THE NAVY.
S.D. JACKSON

51

–All About Gravy–

A good pan of gravy can inspire poetry. A delicately made sauce turns a good vegetable into a sensation. This is really the time when you can use your imagination. Try a different herb, or use a combination of herbs that you like. My favorite gravy happened by accident when I used chick pea flour instead of whole wheat. On a frosty winter night, what grain is complete without a little gravy on top? Imagine a thick mustard sauce over cauliflower!! I consider a biscuit almost naked if there's not something for it to sop up. Sauces are the way to win the hearts of those meat and potato vegetarians you know. The next time you have your parents over for dinner, make fried chicken tofu with mashed potatoes and gravy; your mother will wonder what she did right for a change.

WHITE SAUCE

Here is the basic recipe for a plain white sauce, from which you can build almost any sauce or gravy.

3 TBS. Margarine, Butter, sesame oil or olive oil
The best gravy always starts with the "drippings" left in the pan. After frying or sauteing something, instead of rinsing out the pan, use it for the base of your sauce. If you have no drippings, use sesame or olive oil to saute the sauce vegies (onions, mushrooms, soy-sage, seeds, or nuts). For a more delicate herb sauce, use only margarine or butter, as oil is a bit heavy, tending to hide the flavors.

3 TBS. Flour
You have many choices here; whole wheat or unbleached white flour are the old standbys. Try chick pea flour, rice flour, or corn meal for a change. Don't forget arrowroot, kudzu, or corn-starch as thickeners.

1 to 1-1/2 cups of liquid
This is a good time to clean out your refrigerator. You may use soy milk or water (only use water as a last resort) that was used to steam vegetables. Tomato juice is delicious. Don't be afraid to stir in some chutney, chilli sauce, sweet and sour sauce, prepared mustard, worcestershire sauce, or hot sauce. Flat beer, wine, or sherry work too.

Those are some of the options; here are a few of the tricks. Melt the margarine over low heat in a cast iron skillet or sauce pan. Make sure it doesn't burn. Add flour and stir until you have a nice paste (you have just done something very French called "making a roux"). Keep on stirring until the flour has had a little time to roast, giving it some flavor. Slowly stir in the liquid, until all the lumps are gone and the mixture starts to thicken. This takes a few minutes of careful attention.

HINTS
ℕº 1

If your sauce just won't thicken, don't despair. In a small bowl, mix with COLD water one TBS. of corn starch or flour until completely dissolved. Add this to the gravy and it should thicken right up.

ℕº 2

If your sauce is thick and lumpy and you are having a hard time stirring, use a good wire whip and make it easy on yourself.

If after all these directions you think this is hard, believe me, it isn't. Instead of washing away the makings of a great gravy, add a handful of flour, a little liquid, and it's magic!

"CHICKEN" GRAVY

The best way to make this is to start with a skillet you just made fried chicken tofu in. It's not easy to make chicken gravy when you don't have a chicken. It's even harder if you don't have any tofu, or something greasy in the bottom of your skillet just to get you started. This is the recipe I have come up with and it literally brings tears to my eyes. I was weaned on chicken gravy.

YOU'LL NEED:
1 big handful flour
1/3 stick butter
several pinches salt
1 to 3 cups soy milk, milk or rice milk
hard boiled egg chopped up
1/4 cup nutritional yeast

Generously cover the bottom of a cast iron skillet with flour (use white or whole wheat; the best is a combination of white and chick pea flour). Put this over low heat. The secret of this is to let the flour brown very slowly. Stay close at first; you won't have to stir very much. After a few minutes just stand there and stir away. Add the nutritional yeast now and keep stirring. If you have any Cancer in your astrological chart, you will love making gravy, stir till your heart's content. This should not happen too fast. If the flour should begin to brown too quickly or start to burn, turn the heat down, it's up too high. You want a nice golden brown. Add butter and keep stirring, it should make a nice paste. Pour in warm milk or soy milk slowly, and add salt while continuing to stir. The lumps will go away. By this time you should stop using a wooden spoon and start using

a whip. Congratulations to all the girls who already knew that. Now is the time to get any and all of the lumps out. Depending on how thick you like your gravy, determines how much liquid you pour in. If you want it thinner use more milk, if not, don't use as much in the beginning. Chop the egg and add it along with lots of fresh grated black pepper. That's it! You can taste it now and see if it needs more salt or a dash of tamari. This is a recipe that is not to fancy sort of like what Ma Joad made for her family on the way to Califor-nia. Best when ladled over biscuits, rice, or mashed potatoes, this gravy is good on anything.

P.S. If you have just cooked anything in your skillet and there's something left such as bits and pieces of onions (drippings), then that is the best time to make gravy. Don't let this go to waste, add a handfull of flour directly to the skillet and follow my directions.

P.P.S. IF YOU DON'T EAT EGGS... then good for you, here's another way to make it. Add 1/4 cup sesame seeds to flour in the beginning and let roast together. Follow the regular directions from there and just omit the egg.

Mushroom ∞Gravy∞

1/4 to 1/3 stick of butter (or oil)
2 cups chopped mushrooms
1 small onion chopped small
1 big handful flour
2-3 cups soy milk or milk
tamari, salt, and pepper to taste

Saute the onions and mushrooms in butter until soft. Add flour and stir (at low heat) until a paste forms and the flour has had time to brown a little. Add soy milk and continue stirring with whip or a fork until the mixture thickens. Add more or less liquid depending on the consistency you want. A touch of tamari, salt, and lots of black pepper and it's ready to pour over rice, potatoes, biscuits, and even toast!!

MRS. MARONI'S PESTO

1 cup olive oil- as needed
1 to 3 cups equal amounts fresh basil leaves and spinach or parsley - picked over - big steams cut off (You may use spinach leaves or parsley, but the taste is very different. Basil makes the true pesto.)
2 or 3 cloves garlic
1/4 cup pine nuts or walnuts
1/4 cup grated parmesean cheese
(optional, but really good)

Chop very fine, the basil and spinach or parsley, into a food processor. Next add garlic, then parmesan. While food processor is going, add oil slowly in a thin stream. The mixture should have a thick, buttery consistency. Serve this immediately over fresh, hot pasta. Don't ladle it over the noodles like you would tomato sauce—just a dab should do. It's an intense condiment and good on salad or added to minestrone or lentil soup. It is positively sensuous and can't be recommended highly enough. When I serve this to guests, I ask one of them to pick the basil from the patch in the garden or the window box.

P.S. To store pesto, put in a small jar and cover with a film of olive oil. Use an airtight lid and keep in the fridge.

P.P.S. You may want to use more or less oil, basil, or parsley to your taste. The first few times you make this it won't hurt to add a little at the time of each ingredient until you get the hang of it.

A FAIL SAFE HEADACHE
~HANGOVER~
~UPSET STOMACH~
~ACID STOMACH~
COLD CURE

1 TBS. Kudzu
1 cup cold water
touch of tamari
one umboshi plum or pit
fresh ginger juice (best for colds only)

Dissolve the kudzu into the cold water and put over medium heat. Stir very slowly with a wooden spoon, just to keep the lumps out. Watch closely, when it turns from a watery, milky liquid to a slightly thickened transparent stuff it's done. This is pretty subtle, but if you're watching you'll notice. Pour into a cup and add 1 or 2 tsp. of tamari, according to your taste. Now add an umboshi plum. I usually use the meat of the plum in a sauce or sushi and put the pit back in the jar to use for this reason. So use the whole plum or just the pit, which ever you want.

If you have a cold add between 1 tsp. and 1 Tbs. fresh grated ginger juice. This depends on how big your cup is and if it's for an adult or child etc. This won't stop your cold, but it will help your throat, chest, nose, and all that other good stuff. (Chances are if you haven't been eating dairy products, you won't catch a cold.)

This is really a wonder drink and I've seen it cure some real dillies.

P.S. It helps to suck on the umboshi pit after you've finished the drink. If you can't find umboshi plums at your health food store (or the ones you find are too expensive) look in a little oriental market. Even the tiniest, funkiest ones usually have these at a much cheaper price.

Mario's Hot Sauce

1 Cucumber (peel if waxy and bitter)
3 to 8 Jalapeno Peppers (depending on how hot you like it)
2 Medium Green Peppers
1 Onion, chopped very fine (Red Onions are the best)
2- 12 oz. can of tomatoes (without juice) or 4 to 5 fresh-seeded
1/2 cup fresh cilantro (finely chopped)
Mario says never substitute this; it's the difference between a ten dollar hooker and a high priced call girl.

Blend the cucumber and jalepenos in a blender until you have a very smooth liquid. Chop the green pepper, onion, and tomatoes very fine. Put in a bowl and stir in cucumber/jalepeno mixture along with the coriander. Eat this immediately.

Mario is a very picky eater. He won't eat a thing unless it has hot sauce on it. He perfected the above recipe and we both swear by it.

P.S. Put a touch of honey in the blender with the cukes and peppers if you like your sauce sweet.

NUTRITIONAL YEAST CHEESE

I got this recipe from the Farm Vegetarian Cookbook.* It is a book I would recommend to anyone who is into trying a dairyless diet. It has lots of good recipes and explains how to make your own soy milk and tofu at home. This is a recipe I don't know what I would do without. It substitutes in any Italian dish like lasagna, zucchini parmesan, or even pizza. It's a good topping for stuffed peppers, hot sandwiches, or just plain with rice or biscuits. I like to steam a whole cauliflower and ladle this sauce over it. It also makes a great base for a casserole.

1 cup Nutritional Yeast Flakes
1/3 cup flour
1 1/2 tsp. salt
2 cups water
1/4 to 1/2 cup margarine
1/2 tsp. garlic powder (optional)
2 tsp. wet mustard optional

Mix the dry ingredients together in a pan. Gradually add the water while stirring with a whisk. Make a smooth paste and continue adding the water until it's all used up. Place over heat and stir constantly until the sauce starts to thicken and bubble. Let it cook about 30 more seconds. Remove from the heat and stir in the margarine and mustard.
If you want a thicker, stretchier cheese do this: Substitute 3 TBS. corn starch and 1 TBS. flour for the amount of flour called for. Use 1 cup of oil instead of margarine and add as much as 1 cup

*Farm Vegetarian Cookbook. The Book Publishing Co. 156 Drake Lane, Summertown, Tennessee 38483

more water at the end. Whatever is needed to make a smooth, pourable sauce.
When using Nutritional Yeast be sure you have the right thing. Brewer's yeast and torula yeast do not taste the same. Besides the fact that this is delicious, it has more B vitamins than just about anything else I can think of.

Don't feel like you have to be deprived if you go non-dairy; I have used this in place of cheese successfully everytime I have made it. It's the best.

Swami Rudi Toot-Toot Chutney

It was dog days in August and I had just cleaned up the kitchen for the day. Ralph was standing in the doorway holding a bushel of peaches. He had been sorting out the ones that were too ripe to send to market. "I just sorted through the last of them, do you think you could use one more bushel?", he asked cautiously.

He managed to get out of the room just as a peach smashed into the door frame where his head had just been.

"And that goes for your cat!" I shouted after him.

Don't get me wrong, it wasn't that I didn't like peaches, I love peaches. I had just made10 peach pies, (4 deep dish), dried 5 lbs. of peaches, baked 2 peach cobblers, and frozen 3 quarts of peach sherbet. I had just about stopped frothing at the mouth when Ralph ran back by the door again and shouted, "What about peach chutney?"

Slowly I turn, step by step, inch by inch. Wait a minute, did he say Chutney?? Now that really threw me for a loop. Chutney?? Not only had I never heard of it, I didn't even know what went in it. I had only vague memories of the expensive aisle at the stupermarket; dark jars with red seals and some sort of a testimonial by a Major Grey. Hating to sound as unsophisticated as I felt, I sauntered suspiciously over to the produce department and said, "Well, O.K., I'll try it." Besides, I hated to think of all those peaches being thrown away.

You are never too old to have fun, and did I have fun making that chutney. And the smell... Cyrus (our janitor and world traveler) came drifting into the kitchen and sniffed, "It's like something I had while passing through northern Ceylon." It was truly exotic as hell, a real treat to my senses. I also enjoy making this because it uses lots of spices that I don't normally use together. So, I really implore you to try this. It's easy and so good on a hot day.

Chutney is a must side dish for any Indian meal and a great dish to have in place of relish or hot sauce. I like it best with a big plate of rice.

4 or 5 pounds of peaches, mangos, or apples you can use any of these alone or any combination as well
2 onions sliced up
2 cloves garlic smashed
2 handfulls raisans
1/2 to 1 tsp. cinnamon
1 TBS. grated and squeezed fresh grated ginger or 2 tsp. dry
1 TBS. black mustard seeds
2 tsp. chili powder
2 tsp. paprika
1 tsp. red pepper
1/2 tsp. allspice
1 1/2 cups brown sugar or molasses

(you may want to adjust this after it cooks)
3/4 cups rice vinegar or balsamic vinegar
(as above you may want to adjust)

Saute the onions and garlic in oil until about 1/2 done, add the mustard seeds and continue cooking until they start to pop. Add the rest of the spices, a little more oil if you need to. Stir around, after a few minutes add the sweetener, and vinegar, the peaches, apples or whatever. Simmer this until it is thickened and the tastes have blended. It should be several hours. When you taste to adjust the sweetener, it should have a a kick to it. If it doesn't, add a pinch more cayenne and a little more allspice.

Let this sit in the fridge overnight, really, the longer the better. It will keep for days covered in the fridge and it preserves well too.

Give the lady what she wants MOST

Guaranteed by Good Housekeeping

TOMATO SAUCE

1/2 cup olive oil
3 onions
2 to 3 green peppers
4 to 5 cloves of garlic
2 to 4 cans tomato sauce (This depends on how much you want to make. It's nice to just go ahead and make a big batch, this freezes well, so you can always have some on hand when you want to make pizza or lasagna.)
basil
oregano
whole anise (1 tsp)
one sm. can of tomato paste
1 pinch of cinnamon (optional)
salt and pepper
1 or 2 bay leaves
2 to tsp. paprika
1 can whole tomatoes (optional)

Get the biggest pot you have (preferably cast iron) and a good apron. Pour about 1/2 the olive oil into the pot and let it start to get hot. Please do not even try to substitute any other oil in this recipe; it's got to be olive! While it's heating, slice the onions in thin crescents, slice half the green peppers in long skinny strips and the other half in the tiniest pieces you can. Peel the cloves of garlic and smash them and chop them up. Put all this in the oil and give it a good stir with a wooden spoon. Turn down the heat a little and leave it alone for a few minutes. When you think the onions and peppers are getting soft, add the basil and oregano. I usually use 1 good sized TBS. of basil and oregano each for 2 cans of tomatoes. Remember, you can't use too much of either. Consider it a chance to over come your cautious nature. You may want to put in some more olive

oil now too. Crush the anise and add it too; if you don't have a mortar and pestle that's okay, use wax paper and a ketchup bottle. Definitely do this- It does the same for your spirits as it does for your sauce. Let all this cook for a few minutes, the onions and peppers should be done by now.

Stir in the paste (if you are using whole tomatoes put them in now and mash them up with a potato masher. Next pour in tomato sauce. Stir in bay leaves, salt, and pepper. If you like a sweet sauce, add a tiny pinch of cinnamon, if not, leave that out. Add paprika and about 1 empty can of water.

Make sure the heat is turned down and the lid is on the pot slightly ajar (this cuts the acidity). Simmer about 2 to 4 hours. Adjust taste after first hour or so. Stir only occasionally. If it needs a kick add a pinch or so of cayenne.

This tomato sauce comes out differently every time I make it. It is great with pasta alone or as a sauce for any Italian dish, stuffed peppers, or stuffed cabbage leaves. I like to scrape the bottom of the pot with a big piece of garlic bread. If you have any left over, remember to freeze it and enjoy it twice!

Company Tomato Sauce

When you think you need a heavier sauce, for spaghetti maybe- this is a nice way to do it.

While the sauce is cooking, in another skillet crumble and brown on all sides 1/2 pound or so of soy-sage. When this is pretty crispy, or as brown as you like it, add the sliced mushrooms (leave the little ones whole). Simmer until tender, when it's ready add the whole skillet plus juice to the tomato sauce.

I make this extra step, because if I try to cook every thing together in one pot, it all gets sort of mushed up and nothing cooks the way it should. I have very good results doing it this way and best of all, Tommy Adorni used to stagger into the kitchen, empty plate in hand, tears in his eyes, lick the side of the pot and confess, "this tastes just like my grandmother's!"

WHITE WOMAN'S BAR-BE-QUE SAUCE

3 onions thinly sliced
2 cloves garlic smashed and chopped
1/3 cup oil
2 to 3 cans tomato sauce (depending on how much your pot will hold and how many you are feeding)
3/4 cup molasses
2 TBS. brown sugar (if you don't want to use sugar it's okay to omit, but it makes a subtle difference)

1 tsp. all spice
1 tsp. chilli powder
1/2 tsp cayenne
1/2 cup prepared mustard (yellow)
juice from half a lemon (if you have it around)
1 TBS. fresh grated ginger juice (see end of recipe)
2 TBS. brown rice miso dissolved in 1/2 cup water
2 TBS. tamari
salt to taste

Saute onions in oil; when soft add all spice, cayenne, then molasses and mustard. Stir around, then add miso dissolved in water. Cool a few more minutes then add the rest of the ingredients. Let it simmer a few hours. After it cooks awhile, taste and add more all spice or cayenne if it needs a kick. Maybe a touch more molasses? That's it.

This is the best bar-be-que sauce I've ever had. It's a must for any outdoor to-do. Make a lot because people will come over and ask you for a whole bowl to eat with their dinner.

A NOTE ON FRESH GRATED GINGER

Grate ginger on the fine edge of your grater until you have about one loosely packed 1/4 to 1/2 cup. (Do this on the fine side, not the tiniest one though.)

You can be fancy if you want to and put this in a cheese cloth and squeeze out the juice, but I usually just put it in my hand and give it a real hard squeeze. You can squeeze this right over the pot or into a spoon if you want to measure exactly. Fresh ginger juice is the secret of a lot of my recipes and the taste simply cannot be duplicated. If you have to use powdered, use 1 TSP.

ENCHILADA SAUCE

The moon was in Scorpio and I was three sheets to the wind. A huge pot of beans had been simmering on the stove, oil was popping in a big skillet and Tommy Merritt had just given me a second wink from across a big bowl of hot sauce.

"The secret is to just pretend you're making Mexican gravy." I watched as he dumped a bunch of onions into the oil and shook long black curls out of his face. He turned, sexual waves coming at me like mig bombers; he told me about Paris and the red-headed stranger and poured me another glass of Mouton-cadet. The onions sizzled, he threw in some herbs, by this time the smell was incredible.

"Hey, pour in some of that bean juice, would you?" He was stirring and I was rolling another joint.

"Yeah, my mamma always let me stir the gravy when I was little." He dipped his finger in the sauce and swore at not being able to get anything hot enough this far from home.

Then Tommy threw back his head, rocked back on one heel, and spun around three times (a feat at which he's at the top of his field). He grabbed

me and whispered into my ear, "The incredible thing about magnets is that they work even in outer space... and that's where we are, baby, outer space."

1/3 cup oil
1 to 2 onions, chopped
2 cloves garlic, smashed and chopped
1 TBS. chilli powder
1/4 tsp. cayenne
1 to 2 TBS. savory
1/3 cup flour
about 3 cups liquid (use 1 part tomato juice to one part bean juice or water)
salt and pepper

Heat oil in skillet, add onions and cook a minute or two, and then add herbs. Let them cook with the onions, it helps bring out the flavor. Add flour and stir til brown but not burnt. Add more oil or a little butter if you need to. Stir until there are no real "lumps" and the onions are soft. Add whatever liquid you are using and stir until thickened. Add salt to taste. Enjoy over any Mexican dish; burritos, enchiladas, rice, quesadillas, or corn bread.

One Kind of Sweet and Sour Sauce

1 pineapple cut into chunks or 1 can of pineapple chunks
1/3 cup pineapple juice or water
2 green peppers sliced into long skinny strips
2 to 3 TBS. corn starch
3 TBS. oil
2 cloves garlic smashed
1/2 cup rice vinegar
1/3 cup maple syrup or brown sugar
1/2 onion chopped up
1 TBS. tamari
1/2 tsp. salt
1 tsp. powdered ginger or 2 tsp. fresh grated juice

Heat oil in a skillet, add onions and garlic and let cook until about half done. Add pineapple chunks, vinegar, maple syrup, ginger, and green peppers last. This should not be turned up too high.

Dissolve the cornstarch or kudzu in as small amount of cold water as possible. Add this to the reserved pineapple juice. If you had no juice, it's okay to just use cold water. Stir this around slowly in the skillet and it should start to thicken right up. Add tamari and a touch of salt. Keep stirring over low heat until it looks about right. This is a delicious sweet and sour and it's good with deep fried tempeh sticks, big bowls of rice, steamed or broiled tofu, stir-fried vegetables, or any oriental dish.

Another Kind of Hot Sweet and Sour

This wins the world record for weird ingredients in a recipe, but it's so good and it's very easy. After having it once, I started craving it with every Chinese dish I ate. It is perfect for egg rolls or fried tempeh. If you get into hot foods you'll be addicted.

1 cup or 1 sm. jar pineapple or apricot preserves
1/3 cup horseradish
3 to 4 TBS. dry mustard
(taste after 3 and see what you think)

Mix it all up in a small bowl and chill. If you are having a Chinese diner, you won't need another condiment besides this and soy sauce with a few gratings of fresh ginger in it.

HERBS <u>AND</u> *SPICES*

Herbs are, of course, a world unto themselves. Fortunes were built around them; continents were discovered in search of them; many a heart was won at a mere whiff; forbidden universes were revealed by the taste of them.

If you are serious about learning to cook, you might as well plunge in. Don't be skimpy or cautious with herbs- it's good to make mistakes. That's the only way of finding out what you like.

Once I accidently filled up my pepper grinder with coriander pods. It was a while before I figured it out but I learned a lot about coriander. Cayenne, I found, if added to food without cooking, makes it taste hot right away. If it cooks, the longer it simmers, the longer it takes the kick to come (it will really creep up on you believe me!). The tiniest pinch of tumeric will turn almost any food yellow. You can add a fresh herb leaf (purple basil, dill, tarragon) to a bottle of white wine or rice vinegar and make a very exotic salad dressing.

Experimenting is what makes cooking exciting; herbs and spices are a sure road to adventure. It's a way of living dangerously without ever having to leave your kitchen- except to make a quick trip to the herb garden.

WHAT'S THIS ABOUT KUDZU?

If you are wondering, when I say kudzu, if I could possibly mean those green vines that have totally taken over the Deep South and the better part of Virginia, Tennessee, and the Carolinas, yes, that is exactly what I mean. Although what you buy at the health food store is imported from Japan, and the root has been processed, it is the same thing. Orientals have been using kudzu as a thickener for years, centuries even. Not only is it a wonderful thickener, it has lots of healing properties. Read the ingredients on headache cures. Kudzu is also good for ulcers and intestinal problems. Why hasn't some young enterprising, vegetarian entrepreneur cornered the kudzu market here in America? I bet Southern Environmental Agencies would pay you to pull it up for them.

PIES

"BUT WHEN THE SUN
IN ALL ITS STATE
ILLUMED THE EASTERN SKIES,
SHE PASSED ABOUT THE
KITCHEN GATE
AND WENT TO MAKING PIES."
PHOEBE CARY 1824-1874

HINTS ABOUT PIES

There is something about the "mystique" of a good pie that fascinates me. The picture of a little house with a thatched roof and rose garden is just not complete without a couple of pies cooling on the window sill.

Loretta Lynn had won 18 (or was it 22) blue ribbons at the county fair before she ever had a gold record. Marybelle Morgan has already compiled the statistics: ask any American man what he wants for dessert and he'll say PIE 80% of the time. If he's white, he'll more than likely say apple, and if he's black he'll probably say sweet potato.

The recipe hardly ever varies, but ask any cook and she'll say, "Now there's a trick to it..." And of course, no trick is ever the same. I nearly drove myself crazy trying to make the perfect pie crust. Remember, pies aren't just for dessert; there's quiche, pizza, vegetable pie, and deep dish country pie, to name a few. If you can master the crust, the filling is a cinch. Here is every secret and trick I've ever heard of or come up with myself: the zen of pie...

NO 1 If you are making a traditional pie crust, start off on the right foot and use whole wheat pastry flour. The gluten has been removed from it...that's what makes it pastry flour. Gluten is what makes the dough be all sticky and gooey, like what happens when you make bread, not pie crust.

NO 2 It is my personal opinion that any shortening that is consumed by me goes directly to my thigh in the form of a big lump of cellulite. (And it remains there forever!) You might be asking yourself, what this has to do with pie crust...well, in my experimenting, a lot of real heavy-duty pie makers told me to use Crisco to get a perfect pie crust. In my relentless search, I admit, I tried it. The pie was good, great even, but as I was cleaning up something very strange happened. (I had heard that a food processor worked well for making pie crust, instead of cutting the shortening in by hand.)

While washing the dishes, I noticed that there was a big blob of shortening stuck in the cylinder opening on the lid of the machine. I couldn't reach it with my hand so I figured I would just melt it off with real hot water. I held that thing under the steaming hot water for almost ten minutes and couldn't believe my eyes. It was the immovable force—no wonder my thighs looked the way they did. It was the original blob. After stabbing it with a long skinny knife, I finally loosened its grip. So does that mean I'm going to have to stab myself in the thigh to really look good in a bathing suit??? Anyway, those are the scientific facts. Use what ever you want: butter, margarine, oil, shortening, or soy margarine. They all work more or less the same, but don't say I didn't warn you.

Nº 3 The one thing that all cooks agree on is this: handle the pastry as little as possible. This includes stirring and rolling out.

Nº 4 When you are rolling out the pastry, do it between 2 sheets of waxed paper. It will keep the dough from sticking to the table and you can just pick the whole thing up and flip it right into the pie plate. Also, when you do this, put a couple of drops of water under the waxed paper to keep it from slipping around while you're trying to roll.

Nº 5 The first couple of times that I made pies, right after I got the dough in the plate, I would get real excited and pinch the sides of the crust into fancy designs. Then after I got the filling in and the top layer of crust on I would realize—wait a minute, you aren't supposed to pinch the sides until last so you can pinch the top and bottom together. (Don't make that dumb mistake!)

Nº 6 Always make sure you use ice water.

Nº 7 Remember to pre-heat your oven; start your pie in a very hot oven (400^ to 425^) and turn it down after about 15 minutes. The cold dough in a hot oven makes the dough puff into a very light flaky pastry and that is what you are after.

Nº 8 If you aren't going to use your dough right away then refrigerate it. (It's best to chill at least one hour anyway.) If you leave it in the fridge a long time, let it sit out about one hour before you try to roll it out.

Nº 9 When you put the filling in a pie don't be afraid to heap it in— remember it will cook down a bit.

Nº 10 If you are baking a pie crust by itself, don't forget to prick the bottom. If the air can't escape it will make a bubble in the crust.

Nº 11 Some people say you should brush the bottom of your crust with egg white or milk so it won't get soggy. I never have milk or eggs around so I use soy milk or egg replacer; both work fine. I only do this with real juicy pies like blueberry or cherry.

AUNT SALLY DYER'S BASIC PIE CRUST

2 cups whole wheat pastry flour
1 tsp. salt
2/3 cup margarine
5 TBS. or less ice water

Stir the flour and salt into a bowl. Cut in the margarine. Do this with a pastry cutter, 2 knives cutting against each other, or even the tips of your fingers. Do this until the pastry is somewhere between the texture of cornmeal and peas. Barely sprinkle the dough with ice water, don't put it all in at once, just a few spoonfulls at a time. Stir it quickly with a fork; as soon as you can make it hold together in a ball it's done.

You can roll it out now, but it's best to refrigerate it for an hour ar so. (It can be left in the fridge for about a week.) When ready to roll out, divide into 2 pieces. Roll between 2 pieces of wax paper. Try not to use much more flour. Roll from the center of the pie outward. Pull off top sheet of paper and turn into pie plate. Now it's ready to be filled. You can make a lattice crust, or roll out another piece to place over the entire pie. Cut a little design in the top if you'd like, or just prick with a fork.

If the pie is to be baked unfilled, flute edge and either prick bottom with fork, or put in a hand full of dry beans. Bake at 425^ for 12 to 15 minutes or until light brown. This recipe makes one pie with top and bottom crust or 2 shells.

PUMPKIN PIE WITH OATMEAL CRUST

4 cups pumpkin, butternut, buttercup, acorn squash
1 cup apple juice
1/3 cup maple syrup plus 2 TBS. molasses or brown sugar
1/2 tsp. salt
1 tsp. cinnamon
1/2 tsp. powdered ginger or 1 tsp. fresh grated juice
pinch cloves or all spice (about 1/4 tsp.)
3 portions egg replacer
1 tsp. vanilla
1/2 cup chopped pecans or walnuts

Cut squash into chunks, simmer in apple juice until soft. Put in blender with rest of ingredients, blend till very smooth. If it seems like it needs to be a little firmer add another spoon of egg replacer. Pour this into a pie shell. Sprinkle top generously with chopped pecans, walnuts, or black walnuts. Bake at 350^ for 25 to 30 minutes. Let sit awhile before cutting. This pie is incredible and so much better made with real squash instead of canned pumpkin.

OATMEAL CRUST

1 1/2 cups oats
3/4 cups whole wheat pastry flour
1/2 tsp. salt
1/3 cup margarine, safflower oil, or sesame oil
1/2 cup cold water

Roast oats over a slow flame until they are lightly browned and you can smell them. Mix the oats in a bowl with the flour and salt or put in a processor for a finer crust. Add oil and stir well with a fork. Add water a little at a time. Let sit about 20 minutes then add pumpkin or squash. Bake whole pie at 350 for about 30 minutes. An oatmeal pie crust is good with most any fruit or vegetable pie.

P.S. 1 or 2 TBS. dark rum is a good addition to pumpkin pie; add with vanilla.

APPLE PIE WITH RYE CHEDDAR CRUST

5 or 6 cups sliced baking apples
1/3 cup honey
pinch salt
1 TBS. corn starch or arrow root

Core and slice apples. Only peel them if you want to; it's not necessary though. Toss the apples with the honey, corn starch, and salt. Turn into rye cheddar crust and dot with butter or margarine. Cover with upper crust and pinch sides together. Prick a few holes in the top. Bake at 425^ the first 10 minutes, then turn down to about 350 and bake about 35 minutes, or till done.

RYE CHEDDAR CRUST

3/4 cup rye flour
3/4 cup whole wheat pastry flour
1 tsp. salt
1 cup sharp cheddar cheese
1/3 cup margarine
1/4 cup ice water, or enough to make pastry hold

Mix the dry ingredients together in a bowl then cut in the margarine and cheese. Add cold water to make it hold. Chill one hour then roll out. Remember to prick bottom.
This is a real indulgence and worth every bite. It is also good pastry for vegetable pies.

ELEANOR DARE'S MINCE MEAT PIE

1 cup raisins
1 cup currants
2 cups chopped pineapple
1/2 cup honey or maple syrup
1 cup molasses
1 or TBS. grated orange peel
1 orTBS. grated lemon peel
3 cups chopped apple
1 cup cider
1 tsp. cloves
1 tsp. cinnamon
juice of 1 orange
juice of 1 lemon
1/2 to 1 cup brandy (optional)
pinch salt
1 tsp. nutmeg
1/2 cup walnuts (optional)
3 heaping TBS. brown rice miso

Mix all the ingredients in a pot and start cooking. Dissolve the miso in the apple juice before adding. Don't put the brandy in until the very last. If this seems really watery or runny, dissolve a couple of TBS. of kudzu or corn starch in COLD water and add to mince meat and stir till thickened.

You might want this to mellow in the fridge for a couple of days. Spoon into a 9 inch pie plate with pastry. Make a criss cross crust for the top. Bake at 350^ for about 35 minutes until the crust is done.

Who's Eleanor Dare? The first white woman to give birth in America..to a girl named Virginia.

More Good Things to do to Apple Pie...

1. Use half apples and half green tomatoes. Use the same amount of honey, and a touch of cinnamon. Try a corn meal crust with this. The pie will be a delicacy.

2. Substitute peanut butter for the margarine in a traditional crust. Add a handful of raisins and a pinch of cinnamon to apples.

3. Dissolve 1 or 2 TBS. of miso into as little water as possible, add the juice of half a lemon and toss with apples, honey, and 2 TBS. corn starch or arrow root.

BERRY PIE

She had been stuck outside of Erwin for about three hours and it was getting pretty boring, besides it was getting dark. Licorice had heard about weird things happening here; haunted hollers where gravity'd gone haywire, ant hills bigger than people, and elephants — hung in the dead of night. (I do believe in spooks, I do believe in spooks, I do, I do, I do.)
All day she had been trying to scope out if the passing cars were full of drunk men or lone weirdos before she put out her thumb. But the sun was almost down and this was the land of enchantment.

An old blue Chevy pulled up and stopped about thirty feet down the road. Licorice picked up her stuff, ran down to the car and jumped in the back seat. It was a family of bald headed inbreds drinking Pepsi Colas and eating potted meat from a can; they were going her way. Licorice rolled up her leather like a pillow and laid down her load.

It was a long walk up the road to the house; Licorice was taking her time, picking blackberries along the way. She needed some time to mull over her career and basically, to re-group. Patsy didn't think of her as the famous Licorice of the Licorice Whip and the Bad Boys, but just plain old Licorice. She had always written her best songs in the Minni ha-ha Wash a Rama anyway.

About that time, the dogs heard her and started barking and the commotion brought Patsy out quick. "Honey, where you been?? I dreamed about you last night, I been expecting you all morning."

Licorice put the berries down on the front porch, grabbed Patsy and hugged her like she was the last straw.

Godamn, Patsy, if you're not sweeter than those blackberries!" (Licorice loved to make Patsy blush!). It took me three days to get here, I need some attention!" she demanded.

"That suits me fine," (Patsy mothered Licorice shamefully). "How about we go in the kitchen, I'm going to make you the best berry pie you ever bit into."

4 or 5 cups of berries (blackberry, blueberry, red raspberry, strawberry, huckleberry— or just about any fresh fruit)
2-3 tbs. cornstarch, tapioca or kudzu
1/4 to 1/2 cup honey, depending on sweetness of berries
1 tbs lemon juice (optional)
few tbs margarine of butter
Pie Shell and enough for a top

Wash and pick through the berries. Slice up if you need to. Reserve a bit of the juice and dissolve the corn starch or kudzu into it. Add back to berries with honey and lemon juice, toss and let sit ten minutes. (At this point you could also add a handfull of raisans, a bit of applesauce, or any spice you particularly like: cinnamon, anise, cardamom). Turn into pie shell. Dot with margarine. Cover with other half of pastry or lattice top (which, I will admit when I do it, has driven me insane).

Start this in a hot oven (425 or 450) for about ten minutes, then turn it down and finish it at about 350. It should take about 40 minutes, the crust should be brown and beautiful.
P.S. Don't forget cherries, be sure to get every pit out.

MARGOT CHANNING'S PECAN PIE

1/4 cup margarine or butter
1 1/2 cup chopped pecans
3/4 cup honey, or 1/4 cup maple syrup
and 1/2 cup barley malt
1 TBS. molasses
pinch of salt
1 1/2 cup squash or sweet potatoes
1 cup cold water
2 TBS. kudzu or corn starch
3/4 tsp. ginger
1 tsp. vanilla
pinch of cinnamon

Cream the margarine and the sweetener. In a blender, puree the squash, and in a separate bowl, mix the water and kudzu. When this is dissolved, add it to the stuff in the blender. Add the ginger, cinnamon, and salt. Stir this into the margarine and honey mix and then add the pecans and vanilla. Pour into an unbaked pie shell and bake at 350^ for 40 to 45 minutes until done.

Our Senses Help us Enjoy Food

THE KNOCKOUT PUNCH CHOCOLATE NO CREAM PIE

1/3 cup carob or cocoa powder
1 cup sugar
1/2 tsp. salt
1/3 cup arrowroot flour or corn starch
1 tsp. instant espresso or 1 TBS. instant coffee
1 tsp. vanilla
1 TBS. kahlua or 1/2 tsp. rum extract
3 cups soy milk, coconut milk, or milk
1 pre-baked pie shell
(when you make the crust for this pie, add 1/2 cup of coconut when cutting it)

In a sauce pan stir the cocoa, corn starch, salt, sugar and instant coffee together. Stir in the soy milk (or other milk) over low heat. Let come to a boil and continue to cook about 10 minutes. Stir in vanilla and kahlua or rum. Pour this into a pie shell and let cool. It is completely delicious and unbeatable as a pie or pudding.

A really good crust to use with this pie is this: use natural food graham crackers (there are good ones on the market with no sugar or lard). Crush a couple of packages and mix with one stick melted butter. Press into pie plate.

MOTHER CABRINI'S PIZZA PIE

We used to go to a great place in Denver called Famous Pizza. Up front by the window, the boys had their t-shirts rolled up to show off big arm muscles while they kneaded big hunks of pizza dough. Tattooed Love Boys. Some wild eyed seventeen year old Italian girl would always run by the counter, crying and screaming, "I hate you, I hate you, Tony!" There was an old, mean looking man who slunk around the back, drinking gin from a tall red plastic glass, and leering at anyone who even glanced in his direction. You could never be quite sure what was going to happen there, especially around lunch time, when it got busy.

We liked to go in the afternoon, and I would drink endless cups of coffee while my husband ate piece after piece of onion pizza. Yeah, I loved hanging out at Famous Pizza, but when I'm really in the mood to eat pizza, I make it myself. It's by far the best I've ever had, and here's my step-by-step, all secrets included, recipe.

Start with a good sauce. If you don't already have some, read the tomato sauce recipe. It's easy and can cook while you are making the rest of the stuff.

Here's how to make the crust. This is an easy crust; it doesn't rise so you can have it done in about five minutes.

1 block tofu
egg replacer (equivalent to 2 eggs)
2 to 3 TBS. olive oil
1 tsp. salt
1 1/2 to 2 cups flour (whole wheat is fine)
2 heaping tsp. baking powder

Mix the dry ingredients together and set aside. Put the tofu, oil, and egg replacer in the blender and blend till smooth. Add these to the dry ingredients and mix well. Grease a cookie sheet and also put a lot of oil on your hands. Press the dough into the pan. You may think you have made a mistake, but don't worry, this is a funny dough, real wet and sticky. (If you keep your hands oiled, it will press right into the pan.)

Now ladle the sauce onto the crust. Just put however much you like. You are half finished and doing fine.

If you eat cheese, slice one block of mozzarella cheese into medium pieces and place evenly over the pie. If you don't eat cheese, grate or slice thin spread evenly over the pie one block of mochi (garlic or plain) or fake cheese. This can be found in the frozen food section of your local health food store, or you can read how to make your own mochi in the chapter on grains.

If you are having your pizza plain (I can't imagine), skip on to the next paragraph. If you are going for the Cabrini Su-Preme, read on.
Slice thinly whatever you want on your pie:

GREEN PEPPERS, CRUMBLED SOY-SAGE, BLACK OR GREEN OLIVES, CHOPPED EGGPLANT, MUSHROOMS, ONIONS, SLICED TOMATOES, SQUASH, ZUCCHINI, NUTS

Decide what you want and spread evenly over the cheese or mochi. If you are dairy-less, grate a little more mochi and sprinkle over vegetables. If not, sprinkle about 1/4 cup grated Parmesan over the toppings. Now, and this is the secret, pour a little olive oil into a small bowl. Dip your fingertips into this and drizzle oil over the top of the pie. Don't be stingy here. Crumble and sprinkle 1/2 to 1 TBS. oregano over top of everything. There...isn't it a beautiful masterpiece?

Bake this at 375^ for about 30 to 40 minutes. If you make a real heavy pie, it will take a bit longer. It's done when it pulls away from the sides and the bottom is brown when lifted with a spatula.

Tofu Pot Pie with Cornmeal Crust

1 block tofu, chopped up
2 carrots, sliced thin
1 onion, chopped
1 potato, cooked and diced
1/3 cup flour, any kind
3/4 cup water
2 TBS. miso
tamari
paprika
salt and pepper
1/2 cup sliced mushrooms
1/4 cup sliced toasted almonds (optional)

PASTRY:
3/4 cup pastry flour (whole wheat)
1/2 cup cornmeal
1/3 cup margarine (sesame oil works also)
3 TBS. cold water

Put the potatoes on to boil now, so they will be ready when you need them.

Make the crust next. It can be chilling while you do the rest of the pie. If you don't know how to make a pie crust, read a bit about it before you get started here. Mix the dry ingredients together and then cut in the oil or margarine. Stir while adding the cold water till the dough leaves the sides of the bowl. Wrap in waxed paper till you need it. When I make this, I usually make a fancy criss-cross lattice crust, and leave it at that. It you want a bottom crust also, just double the recipe.

Put about 1/3 cup of oil in the skillet and when it's hot add the flour, salt, pepper, paprika, and onion. Then give it a good stir and turn it down. Dissolve the miso in the water and add to the skillet, stirring until slightly thickened. Then add the chopped vegies, tamari, and nuts. Put in oblong casserole dish with or without bottom crust.

Roll out the crust and cut into long strips. Lay criss-cross over the pie. Bake at 375^ for about 45 minutes or until the crust is brown and the filling is bubbling.

NOLICHUCKY VEGETABLE PIE WITH NUT CRUST

1 to 1 1/2 cups mushrooms
1 onion, chopped
1 or 2 boiled potatoes, cut into small pieces
about 1/2 cabbage, chopped fine
1/2 cup parsley, chopped fine
1 clove garlic, chopped fine
1 or 2 hard boiled eggs (if you eat them)
1 1/2 to 2 cups of your favorite sauce (it can be a non-dairy "cheese" sauce, dill sauce, mustard sauce, onion sesame sauce, cheese sauce, or whatever you like)
salt, pepper, and tamari to taste

If your cupboard is bare and you're having a down-home dinner then go ahead and use potatoes in this recipe. If you are putting on the dog, use artichoke hearts, broccoli, or fresh asparagus.

Saute mushrooms, onions, and cabbage until soft and about half done. Remove from heat and stir in chopped, cooled potatoes, or whatever you're using, and parsley. Then pour into pie shell. If using eggs, slice them and lay over top of pie. Pour a little of the sauce over the pie, not enough to be soggy, but enough so the vegetables won't dry out. If you have any sauce left over, that's good. People usually ask for some to pour over their pie like gravy. Bake in a 350^ oven 30 to 40 minutes or until it's bubbling.

NUT CRUST

2 cups nuts (any combination of the following)
sesame seeds, cashews, pecans
walnuts, brazil nuts, almonds
pumpkin seeds, filberts, peanuts
sunflower seeds

Slightly roast in a skillet (not too much because they'll cook again with the pie). Put in a blender or food processor and grind till about like crumbs. Pour into pie plate. Toss with 1 TBS. of pastry flour and a couple of tsp. of sesame oil (only if it seems dry). Press into plate. This crust is equally good with fruit pies, or chocolate no-cream pie; just toss in a TBS. of honey with the crumbs before pressing into the plate.

CAPTAIN'S COUNTRY PIE WITH BISCUIT CRUST

1 large onion, chopped
2 cups corn, off the cob
1 cup small whole mushrooms
2 to 3 TBS. sesame seeds
3 TBS. nutritional yeast
1 1/2 TBS. corn starch
1 batch baking powder biscuit dough
1 block frozen tofu

Lightly roast seeds in skillet. Add oil and onion and let cook a few minutes, then crumble in thawed tofu. Shake in nutritional yeast and drizzle tamari over the top. Let cook till it's brown all over and it smells real good. Now, add mushrooms and let brown till about half done. Stir in corn last and remove from heat. If this is very dry, dissolve 1 1/2 TBS. corn starch, or same amount of egg replacer. This is always different as you are never quite sure what the vegetables will do. Turn whole mixture into an oblong casserole dish.

Make a biscuit dough as usual. If you want, when you make this you can add chopped parsley, onion, poppy seeds, sesame seeds, even cheese. Roll this out like always. You can cut out biscuits (big ones) and lay on top of casserole, or you can lay the whole dough over top.

Bake in a 400^ to 425^ oven for about 20 to 25 minutes. The top should look just like regular biscuits, nice and brown. If you lift it up with a fork, it should be wet from the sauce, but not doughy. Serve at once with mashed potatoes, gravy, and a green.

Main Courses

What's For Dinner???

New England Boiled Dinner

Nostromo Noodles

Zucchini Parmesan

Tofu Scrambled Eggs

Pocahantas Stuffed Pumpkin

Tofu "Fish" Sandwiches With Tartar Sauce

Tofu Meat Balls

Noodles With Olive Oil And Garlic

Star And Garter Special

Enchiladas

Lame Dog Stew

Sesame Noodles

What About Eggs???

WE MAY LIVE WITHOUT
CONSCIENCE,
AND LIVE WITHOUT HEART;
WE MAY LIVE WITHOUT POETRY,
MUSIC, AND ART;
WE MAY LIVE WITHOUT FRIENDS,
WE MAY LIVE WITHOUT BOOKS;
BUT CIVILIZED MEN CANNOT
LIVE WITHOUT COOKS.
HE MAY LIVE WITHOUT HOPE, —
WHAT IS PASSION BUT PINING?
BUT WHERE IS THE MAN WHO
CAN LIVE WITHOUT DINING??
OWEN MEREDITH 1831-1891

Having to come up with something different to eat three times a day, or even once a day, can be the $64,000 question. It's usually the hardest part of the meal. Dinner parties, brunches, and tea parties are easy to plan; it's those every day meals that make you begin feeling like a hunted rabbit. Don't let trying to figure this out drive you over the edge.

HERE ARE SOME SUGGESTIONS:

№ 1 An empty stomach is the most creative thing in the kitchen. What are you really hungry for??? It's a lot easier to make something if you're craving it. If you're not really hungry you'll never be able to think of anything to cook.

№ 2 What kind of food do you have around? Have you just been to the grocery store, do you have any left-overs, or do you just have an empty pickle jar and some mayonnaise staring at you from an empty fridge?

№ 3 What's the weather like? It's never easy to face a pot of steaming grain on an August afternoon; that's the time for gazpacho. For me, it's always easier to cook something when it's cold out. On the first frosty mornings of fall, wild horses couldn't keep me out of the kitchen. Snowy days inspire soups and breads.

№ 4 Do you feel like making a one dish meal; lasagna or a vegetable pie? Clean out the fridge for a noodle casserole, meat loaf, or burgers.

WHAT'S FOR DINNER???

№ 5 Imagine what it's going to look like on a plate. Aim for a lot of nice colors. Brown: grains, bread, seaweed, beans. Yellow: corn, summer squash, millet, cous-cous. Orange: winter squash, carrots, sweet potatoes. Green: there's every shade from broccoli to nori to artichokes. Want a little red?...try beets, tomatoes, or red cabbage. White: potatoes, tofu, cauliflower. Blue: blue corn meal. Never underestimate the color combination of your meal. Why do you think restaurants put that piece of parsley and orange slice on your plate?

№ 6 Maybe you're just in the mood for sandwiches...

№ 7 If you're just too tired, too hot, too not in the mood, insist that someone else make dinner or take you out. It's never any fun to do anything if you're not into it. If I try to cook something when my heart's not in it, the end result is usually not edible. No meal is more satisfying than one prepared with enthusiasm, love, and guts.

№ 8 Don't be the kind of vegetarian who never eats a vegetable. It is easy to slip into the habit of having a grilled cheese sandwich and potato chips every night but isn't that sort-of missing the point???

№ 9 I have a mental check list that I run through in my head. I call it the balanced plate: a grain, a bean, 2 vegetables, something raw. This is a good way to build a meal, just a little of each group and it's all done.

NEW ENGLAND BOILED DINNER

about 4 potatoes cut into chunks
1 small cabbage cut into quarters or fifths
2 onions, cut into chunks
3 turnips, cut into chunks
2 or 3 carrots, if very small leave whole or cut length-wise, then in half
1/2 to 1 block tofu or tempeh
a big handful chopped fresh parsley
tamari and salt to taste

Pour a little oil in the bottom of a dutch oven or your big soup pot. Let it get hot and add the potatoes, then cabbage and turnips. Add about 1 cup water - enough to keep it from sticking, but not to be like soup. Cover and simmer about 1 1/2 to 2 hours. Use a heat difusor if necessary, and also add small amounts of water if too much evaporation is occuring

Slice tofu or tempeh into a skillet and brown in oil and tamari. Add to pot the last ten minutes of cooking time, or serve as a side dish with boiled dinner. Either is very good. This begs for a nice hot bread of any kind and nothing more. Well...maybe a Guiness or a Harp...

Nostromo Noodles

2 or 3 red bell peppers, sliced and chopped
1 onion, sliced
4 to 6 link soy-sages
(Morning Star Farms is good)
olive oil/ butter
2 cloves garlic, smashed and chopped
1 bag of your favorite ribbon noodle
I love DeCeccio; sesame are good also
salt and pepper
parsley (optional)
1/2 tbs. oregano

Cover the bottom of a cast iron skillet or wok with oil. Heat, then chop up soy-sages and add to oil with onion and garlic. Let cook a few minutes, then add bell pepper. If your noodles aren't already cooked, put your water on and let them cook now. When noodles are done, drain and add to skillet with peppers and onions. Toss gently but try not to stir. Add a few pats of butter now if you want to and some fresh chopped parsley if it's on hand. Cover, turn down, and let heat through. It shouldn't take long. Add salt and pepper and toss again to mix evenly.

I can't emphasize how good this is or how easy it is to prepare. If you can't find soy-sage or don't want to use it, substitute fresh green peas. Add them last.

Zucchini Parmesan

4 or 5 cups good tomato sauce
olive oil
7 or 8 zucchini
1 block tofu, thinly sliced
1 to 2 cups nutritional yeast cheese or fake
cheese
breadcrumbs

This is an easy recipe. Start with a batch of good tomato sauce. Ladle a little into the bottom of a casserole dish and spread around. This will keep it from sticking. Slice the zucchini into medium lengthwise strips. Dip them into the breadcrumbs and lightly saute till tender (doesn't take long). Next, layer the zucchini, nutritional yeast cheese, tofu, then tomato sauce. Continue until all ingredients are used and pan is full. Top with dots of yeast cheese and breadcrumbs. Bake until bubbling in a 350^ oven.

I like to use zucchini instead of eggplant because the zukes are a lot more tender and they don't use half the amount of oil when browning. It makes for a much nicer parmesan.

∞ TOFU ∞ SCRAMBLED EGGS

This is incredible with biscuits and gravy soy-sage, or pancakes. Why wait and have it for breakfast?

1 to 2 lbs. tofu (well drained)
1/4 to 1/2 cup mushrooms
1 cup onion, chopped
1/2 cup green and red bell peppers, chopped small
1/4 cup oil
1/2 cup nutritional yeast
2 TBS. poppy seeds
salt and pepper
parsley
1 TBS. tumeric
2 tsp. thyme
1 clove garlic, chopped
***If you like things hot or a little spicier, add a dash of cayenne or Tabasco.

Saute onions, garlic, mushrooms, and peppers in that order. Add spice and nutritional yeast, lower heat and cook a few more minutes. Crumble in the tofu, stir it in, then add parsley. Let simmer 10 minutes or so. If you think it needs a little more yellow coloring then add more tumeric, but remember the color comes out slowly so don't put in too much.

POCAHONTAS STUFFED PUMPKIN

1 medium pumpkin (cut out the top, scrape out the pulp and seeds, and don't throw away the top)
2 cups bread crumbs
2 cups any left over cooked grain (rice works great)
4 stalks celery, chopped
3 onions, sliced into crescents
1/4 cup toasted sunflower seeds
1/4 cup parsley, chopped fine
1 heaping TBS. sage (you really can't use too much of this, so don't worry about going overboard)
2 tsp. thyme
1/2 cup melted margarine
lots of fresh grated ginger
salt

First of all, make sure that your pumpkin will fit into the oven. Okay, now make a little marinade out of 2 parts oil, 1 part tamari, and a few gratings of ginger. Prick the inside of the pumpkin all over with a fork and pour in the marinade. Turn it all around so that it gets covered.

Saute the onion and celery, and when about half done, add the sage and thyme and cook till you can smell the herbs. It won't take long. Remove from heat and mix everything in a big bowl. If it seems dry, add the melted margarine, if not, just omit it. Stuff all this into your pumpkin and put the lid back on. Sit this in a baking dish or a pie plate, and put it in a 400^ oven for about 1 hour, or until the pumpkin is soft. Serve this immediately, encouraging your guests to take pumpkin along with the stuffing. People get so caught up in the stuffing, they forget that the pumpkin is part of the dinner also, not just a "container."

I love to make this for a big Thanksgiving or Christmas dinner, but most stores stop carrying pumpkins after Halloween. This October, buy two pumpkins, carve one, and keep the other one for a big dinner. It is also nice to get small pumpkins for individual servings.

Tofu "Fish" Sandwiches with Tartar Sauce

1 block tofu
1/2 cup corn meal
oil as needed
buns
tartar sauce

MARINADE:
1/4 cup tamari diluted with
1/4 cup water
2 tsp. kelp
1 tsp. dry mustard
1 clove garlic, pressed
1/4 cup olive oil
good squeeze of lemon juice

Slice tofu and let marinate at least 2 hours.

Spread the corn meal on a plate and coat both sides of the tofu generously with the meal. Pour oil in the skillet. When hot, lay in tofu slices. Fry on both sides until crispy and golden brown. Serve on bun with tomato, lettuce, and lots of tartar sauce. These sandwiches are a little different but the result is absolutely delicious.

Tartar Sauce

1 cup mayonnaise
2 tsp. dijon mustard
3 TBS. sweet relish or sweet pickle (drained)
1 TBS. grated onion
1/4 cup red pepper
juice of 1/2 a small lemon

Mix all ingredients together and enjoy with sandwiches. Keeps really well covered in the fridge.

TOFU MEAT BALLS

Before you make these, read something about making burgers. They're a lot alike.

1 block tofu
2 to 3 cups bread crumbs
1/2 cup parsley, chopped fine
3 medium cloves garlic, chopped fine
1/4 to 1/2 cup nutritional yeast
1 cup grated carrot or zucchini
1/2 cup wheat germ or oatmeal
1 tsp. thyme
tamari or red wine as needed to moisten
salt and pepper

Put all these ingredients together in a bowl and work together with both hands. Roll mixture in the palms of your hands into silver dollar sized balls. Roll balls in whole wheat flour or what have you, fry in hot oil till crispy on all sides.

Don't confine tofu balls to Italian dinners only—they go great with corn bread and beans too. Remember, one of the greatest sandwiches ever is a cold, leftover tofu meat ball sandwich.

NOODLES WITH OLIVE OIL ᴬᴺᴰ GARLIC

This is an easy recipe, and so good that no true Italian restaurant's menu is complete without it. It's exactly what it says it is. If you're into making your own noodles, please do, if not though, sesame ribbons work fine.

1/2 to 1 lb. dry noodles (or however many you need...I never mind having leftover noodles because pan fried noodles is one of my favorite foods)
1/2 to 1 cup olive oil
4 or 5 cloves garlic, chopped and mashed
2 tsp. poppy seeds
2 tsp. oregano (optional)
salt and pepper
condiment of your choice (good tasting nutritional yeast, sesame salt, parmesan, hot sauce, or whatever)

Cook noodles until al-dente. (put about 1 TBS. of oil in the water to cook with them... this keeps noodles from sticking together)

While the noodles are cooking, heat the oil and the garlic in a sauce pan. Let this get very hot, but don't let the garlic burn. Drizzle a little olive oil on the bottom of a large pretty platter.

Drain the noodles and put on a platter or bowl. This always makes me feel like a little Italian grandmother. Pour the oil and garlic over the noodles and toss gently. Sprinkle with poppy seeds. Crush the oregano in the palms of your hands and sprinkle over also. Give another toss and add a little more of everything.

I really love noodles fixed this way. Since it's such an easy recipe, I usually make it when I don't have much time or when I want to spend a lot of time with a salad or dessert.

Dinner at the Star and Garter
OF
Bangers and Spuds
OF
an Evening With Liz

What could be better than a down-home dinner of mashed potatoes and gravy with sausages? There are some delicious vegetarian sausages on the market, as most tofu makers also make there own brand of soy-sage. If you want to try and make this yourself, here's how:

1 block tofu
3 to 4 cups cooked lima beans, navy beans, chick peas, or soy beans
1 cup bread crumbs, chopped very fine
1/4 cup chopped parsley, chopped very fine
1 cold chunk margarine, about the size of an egg
1/4 to 1/2 cup red wine
1 onion, chopped
2 cloves garlic, mashed and chopped
1 TBS. paprika
1/2 tsp. allspice
1/2 tsp. cayenne
2 tsp. thyme
2 tsp. fennel
2 tsp. savory
1 tsp. corriander, crushed
2 tsp. sage
1 egg or egg replacer
and if you like hot stuff, add
1 to 2 tsp. crushed red pepper

The best way to do this is in a meat grinder. If you don't have one, no sweat, just use your hands. Mix all ingredients in a bowl, cover with wine, and let sit in fridge at least 4 hours. If you don't want to use wine, use water diluted with tamari. When ready to use, put through a meat grinder or smash up good with your hands. If it doesn't feel like it's sticking together good enough, add 1/2 cup wheat germ. Shape into patties or links and coat in flour. Fry in hot oil till crispy and brown. This is completely yummy and really not that hard. If you don't have all these spices, that's okay also; just use the ones you have. Any way you slice it, it's still bologna.

If you think this dinner is too funky, get this: I once read that Elizabeth Taylor said this was her favorite dinner. And there's nothing funky about Elizabeth Taylor.

P.S. If you are intent on perfect links, roll out and refrigerate until hard again, then fry.

ENCHILADAS

10 to 12 corn tortillas
1 copy of The Rocky Mountain News
(Tommy Merritt says this paper works
the best, but I guess any will do.)
1/4 to 1/2 cup oil (or as needed)
1 block frozen tofu
1 onion, chopped
1 green pepper, chopped
2 to 3 tsp. cumin powder
1 tsp. chili powder
2 cloves garlic
1 cup chopped black olives
1 cup nutritional yeast cheese
1 batch Tommy Merritt's enchilada sauce
about 1/4 cup tamari
1 or 2 TBS. worchestershire or Pick-a-peppa

Heat oil in skillet, put tortillas in gently one at a time. Just a few seconds on each side. Lay between pages of newspaper.

Let tofu thaw while mixing tamari, pick-a-peppa, cumin, and chili powder in water. There should be about 1/2 a cup of liquid. Crumble the tofu into a bowl, then pour marinade over it.

Heat a little oil in skillet, add chopped onion and green pepper. When half done add tofu and brown. Stir in olives.

Place a large spoonful of tofu mixture into a tortilla. Roll up and place rolled side down in a casserole dish (if you put a few spoonfuls of enchilada sauce on the bottom of the casserole dish before putting the tortillas in, they won't stick). Cover the dish with filled tortillas. Place very close together. Then cover the whole thing generously with enchilada sauce and yeast cheese.

Bake at 375^ for 45 minutes or until very bubbly. Enjoy pronto with any number of things; yellow rice, guacamole, soapillas, or just by themselves. There are all kinds of things you can stuff the enchiladas with besides what I've written. You can use beans, tempeh, vegetables, and/or cheese.

If you are in a hurry, or low on oil, or just trying to cut out some fat from your diet, you can skip frying the tortillas in oil; just roll them up plain.

This recipe is kind of a lot of trouble, but it's worth it. I try to make enough for two meals. Once I get all the stuff out and get going, it's just as easy to fill up two casserole dishes as it is one.

LAME DOG STEW

"Licorice, get out of that hammock and get the broom! It's been trying to rain all day and I want that porch swept before Cody gets here tonight."

"Good God, Patsy, you been going like a buzz-saw since morning. It's not like she's never been here. She musta been out here a million times."

"Not since you ran off with that gui-tar she hasn't. Now go on and finish sweeping." Patsy felt the first drops of rain and looked up at cloudy skies; she wondered if Delores was getting rained on somewhere. She picked up her basket of flowers, remembered the scissors, and went on inside to finish dinner.

Patsy had just finished setting the table when they heard Cody pull up. Licorice hurried out to meet her. Patsy went ahead and got the glasses out of

the freezer and the gin out of the cupboard; she could hear them coming down the hall.

"You look like you just came in off the ark," said Licorice. "Patsy look, she's drenched!"

"She can sit right here by the stove and get warm," said Patsy, "I've got a warm blanket waiting for her."

The three old friends sat and talked a while. There was so much love in the air you could breathe it in.

"I'd hoped Delores would get back for supper, but I'm too hungry to wait any longer. These biscuits won't keep a minute longer," stated Patsy. "Licorice, you sit over here; Cody, you stay close to the stove." Patsy started to bring food out of everything but thin air. Cody couldn't believe her eyes and said, "I haven't seen this much food since you made dinner for the Hill toppers!"

"I know it's a lot," Patsy blushed, "I just wanted to make everyone's favorites." And she sure had. There was stew and collard greens, biscuits, home-made apple butter, potato salad, an onion short-cake with mustard sauce and two big bowls of popcorn and artichokes (Licorice's favorites). By Cody's plate there was a bunch of green onions stuck in a glass of ice water (to keep them crisp) and a dish of sliced tomatoes. There wasn't just a chocolate cake but a rhubarb pie and a big plate of praline cookies to boot.

General dinner time commotion followed. There was much passing of plates and bowls, pickles and hot sauce, exclamations and wild hoots of laughter.

"Damnit, Cody, why won't you join my band?" Licorice asked. "You'll be rich and never have to clean houses again."

Cody took a bite of her onion and rolled her eyes. "You can't fool me...I'd have a pink hair-do before I knew what hit me. And you'll probably try to change my name to Ann Chovy."

"That's great," Licorice yelled as she leapt to her feet. "What a great idea...the boys are gonna love you!"

(Patsy was laughing so hard she had to run to the sink and spit out her coffee.)

"Are you kidding? I saw a picture of you and those Bad Boys; you run with a lame dog," said Cody. "you'll soon learn to limp.."

"Aw come on, they're my friends," said Licorice.

"Yeah, I know," laughed Cody, "that's what scares me."

"Hey, you two, it's stopped raining," said Patsy, "let's finish this pot of coffee and go look for Delores. That damn mare could have had ten foals by now.

3 potatoes, cut into big chunks
3 to 4 carrots, cut lengthwise
2 turnips, cut into chunks
4 red radishes, left whole
1/2 winter squash, cut into chunks
1 block tofu, tempeh, or wheat gluten, marinated and cut up
1 or 2 TBS. miso or vegetable cube, dissolved in cold water
3 TBS. flour, dissolved in cold water (about 1/2 cup water will do)
salt, pepper, tamari to taste

Decide which casserole dish you're going to use. It's got to have a lid. If you don't have one, use an oven proof bowl and aluminum foil. I have a clay baker that I wouldn't trade for anything in the world; it works perfect for this.

Okay, smash 2 cloves garlic and rub all over the bottom and side of the dish. Get vegetables and tofu and cut them up (don't cut them too small; leave them in pretty big pieces). If you want to, arrange the vegies in a pretty design in the dish, or just throw them in any old way. Dissolve the miso and flour in cold water, pour over veggies, add salt, pepper, tamari, and a few dots of margarine. Cover and bake at 350^ to 400^ for an hour or until the vegies are done. 15 extra minutes never hurts. This sounds like a very plain stew; maybe that's why it's so good.

SESAME NOODLES

7 TBS. Dark sesame oil
7 TBS. Tamari
3 TBS. balsamic vinegar
1 TBS. Hot sesame oil
3 TBS. sugar, brown sugar or maple syrup
This is optional, usually I don't put it in.
1 package your favorite noodle
1 bunch chopped scallions
1/2 cup roasted chopped peanuts
This is optional as a garnish

Do you know this recipe? It is so lip smacking good that I stand at the counter with a big fork and eat for about 5 straight minutes the moment I get it mixed together; I go into kind of a feeding frenzy. This is the way I suggest eating sesame noodles, if you are eating with others they should be served cold or at room temperature. This is also a great travelling food.

Put noodles on to cook, while cooking mix together first 5 ingredients in a measuring cup. Pour over drained, hot, cooked noodles, toss in chopped scallions. Sprinkle roasted, chopped peanuts over the top.

Here is a tip. In the recipe don't try to substitute any ingredients. Like using apple cider vinegar instead of balsamic vinegar. If you don't already have these ingredients get them and use them often.

What About Eggs???

Once a wise man said, "Don't look for hidden eggs." For some reason this struck me like a bolt of lightening. When I started this book I didn't eat eggs, but now I put them in fried rice and love it. Nothing smells as bad as a hard boiled egg, but boy, they sure do taste good in potato salad, don't they?

Here is a good recipe for egg replacer that you can make at home. I make a full jar and it seems to last a long time. This will work in any recipe that calls for egg replacer in this book (or probably in just about any one).

Just mix equal parts of arrowroot flour and potato flour. I usually use about 1/2 cup of each, then mix it really well and keep airtight in the fridge. When ready to use, mix 1 TBS. with 2 TBS. water and that equals one egg. There are also several egg replacers on the market right now, all of them pretty good.

SOUPS

A Long Winter's Nap Mushroom Soup

Sarah's Old Time Vegetable Soup

Prem Nagar Pea Soup

Bean Porridge Hot

Boone's Creek Corn Chowder

Solidarity Borscht

How To Make A Cream Soup Without Any Cream

Frogmore Gumbo

Gazpacho

Palumbo's Provincetown Mushroom Barley

Miso Soup

Backroads Lentil Soup

Broccoli Cheddar

Potato Soup

Croutons

Dumplings

"WHERE HEARTS WERE HIGH
AND FORTUNES LOW,
AND ONIONS IN THE STEW."
CHARLES DIVINE 1889-1950

"PLEASE, SIR,
I WANT SOME MORE."
CHARLES DICKENS 1812-1870

LONG WINTER'S NAP MUSHROOM SOUP

4 or 5 cups chopped mushrooms
(leave small ones whole)
2 onions, sliced in crescents
4 TBS. sesame oil (or 1/2 stick margarine)
1/2 tsp. thyme
2 cloves garlic
1 TBS. sesame seeds
2 TBS. tamari
2 TBS. nutritional yeast
6 cups broth or vegetable water
1 carrot, chopped into matchsticks
1/4 to 1/2 cup flour (whatever you've got will
do, but white or rice flour is the best)
1 cup soy milk

Saute mushrooms and onions in sesame oil. Add
garlic, thyme, sesame seeds, tamari, and the yeast.
When the mushrooms are done, add the flour, stirring until brown. Pour in the liquid and let it simmer for one hour. Then 15 minutes before serving,
add the soymilk. If you can't get soymilk, combine
a cup of the soup with half a block of tofu in a

blender. When smooth, add back to the soup. Add
parsley as a garnish, with a few pats of butter and
serve in big bowls with butter milk biscuits. Then
settle down...

SARAH'S OLD TIME VEGETABLE SOUP

1 onion, sliced thin
3 to 4 cloves garlic, smashed
7 cups water
3 potatoes, diced
1 or 2 stalks celery, chopped
1 or 2 carrots, sliced in thin rounds
1 small bunch of your favorite greens
(1/4 to 1/2 head of cabbage works well)
1 medium size jar of tomato or vegetable juice
1 bay leaf
salt and pepper (this likes a lot of salt)
1/4 sesame oil
1/4 -1/2 package your favorite noodles

Saute the onion and garlic in oil until soft. Add the
water and drop in the bay leaf. Put in potatoes,
carrots, celery, cabbage, and greens in that order.
Let simmer one hour or until potatoes are done.
The secret of this soup is never to let it come to a
boil. Now it's time to add the noodles. If they're
not already cooked, it's okay; just give them about
30 minutes to cook. Add the tomato juice, salt and
pepper and let simmer about 30 minutes. Serve
with cornbread. If there are any leftovers, all the
better; this soup is always better the next day.

Once my friend Dorita told me she made this soup
with 12 cloves of garlic. I was incredulous until I
tried it myself; it was great and definitely kept
away the werewolves.

Prem Nagar ❧ Pea Soup ❧

3 TBS. sesame oil 2 light 1 dark
2 to 3 cups dried split peas
2 or 3 times as much water
2 carrots, diced
2 onions
2 cloves garlic, mashed
1 stalk celery
1 bay leaf
1/4 to 1/2 tsp. cayenne
2 TBS. tamari
1 heaping TBS. ground cumin
1 TBS. chili powder
(this adds a very nice flavor without
making it hot)
salt and pepper to taste
toasted sesame seeds

Pour the oil in your soup pot. When it's hot add
the onion and garlic. When these are soft add the
cumin, chili powder, tamari, and cayenne. Stir until
the spices give the mixture a nice aroma. Add the
peas and water. Simmer until the peas are soft and
the mixture is thick. Add more water if you have
to. Top with ground toasted sesame seeds.

I prefer this version of pea soup over the more all-
American varieties. Served with dumplings, it just
can't be beat. Corn bread ain't too bad either

2 or 3 cups dried beans (navy, october,
or any white bean)
3 stalks of celery, chopped
2 cloves garlic, smashed
1 or 2 bottles of flat dark beer
3 TBS. miso, diluted in 1 cup broth or water
2 tsp. dry mustard
1 TBS. honey
salt and pepper

Soak the beans overnight. Rinse well with water,
cover and simmer 2 to 3 hours. About an hour
before they are done add the beer, chopped celery,
onions, and mustard. Let this cook about 30 minutes, then dip out some broth and dissolve miso in
it. When smooth, add back to soup. Add salt and
pepper. Turn the heat down to a simmer; you don't
want the soup to burn. With a potato masher,
mash at the mixture a few times until it's thickened. Let cook another 30 minutes, stirring occasionally. serve with big, crunchy croutons.
It's best when the frost is on the pumpkin.

Boone's Creek Corn Chowder

2 to 3 TBS. sesame or safflower oil
2 cloves garlic, smashed and chopped
one carrot, sliced into matchsticks
4 potatoes, cubed
1 or 2 handfuls of rice
1 onion, chopped
2 stalks celery with leaves, chopped
1/4 tsp. cayenne
4 or 5 ears corn
salt and pepper
1 or 2 TBS. miso (yellow or white is good)

Heat the oil in the pot and add garlic, onion. When slightly cooked, add potatoes and water to generously cover. When potatoes are at least 1/2 done add the rest of the ingredients. Cut corn off 3 cobs, directly over the pot. Take the other 2 ears and break into 2 or 3 pieces; add to the soup like that. Dissolve the miso into a cup of the broth and add back to the soup. Simmer about 1 more hour or 1 1/2 hours.

You can add a cup of soy or plain milk if you want, but it doesn't need it. Maybe a good shake of good tasting nutritional yeast.

When you serve this break a piece of corn on the cob into 3 pieces and put a piece of corn in each person's bowl, and a big plate of biscuits in the middle of the table.

SOLIDARITY BORSCHT

5-7 small beets (without tops)
1 carrot, grated or chopped small
1 onion, sliced fine
5 or 6 cups of water
1 to 3 TBS. honey
1 to 5 TBS. vinegar (I use balsamic vinegar)
or red wine
1 bay leaf
salt and pepper

Wash beets and cover with water and cook till soft. (Leave ends on beets while cooking). When beets are soft, remove from water and set aside. Add other ingredients (carrot and onion) and continue to simmer. Spear beet with knife or fork and run under cold water; the skin should slip right off. Cut the ends off now, discard, and cut the beets into matchstick size. Add back to soup pot. It's about time to remove from heat. Stir in honey and vinegar. I like a little more vinegar; do this to your own taste. Cover and put in fridge. When ready to serve, add 1/2 of a hot potato or a huge dollop of sour cream. This soup absolutely cannot be beaten on a hot day. It cools and refreshes.

How to Make a Cream Soup Without Using Any Cream

The easiest thing to do is to use soy milk; it substitutes perfectly in any milk recipe. Some stores don't have it but most health food stores do. Try oriental food stores; lots of times, they make it fresh. Here are some other ways:

NO 1 Half (mash) at the soup several times with a potato masher, this will thicken it up.

NO 2 Put 1 or 2 cups of the soup in the blender till smooth and stir back into soup.

NO 3 Put 1 or 2 cups of the soup in the blender with 1/2 or so block of tofu and blend till smooth. Stir back into the soup. This is sort of the equivalent to stirring in sour cream.

NO 4 Throw in a handful of rice. Usually if the soup is nice and thick you won't miss the milk.

NO 5 Use nut milk. It's easy to make. Throw 1/4 to 1/2 cup of nuts (any kind tastes good peanuts, almonds, cashews, sunflower seeds...) into a blender with 1 or 2 cups of water; blend till smooth. This substitutes great in most every recipe for cow's milk. It's good too in breads or casseroles.

NO 6 Make a batch of nutritional yeast cheese or a white sauce and stir that in.

NO 7 Eat a nice clear soup like miso more often!

NO 8 To make low fat sour cream: line strainer with paper towel plop yogurt in and put over bowl. Let strain overnite in fridge.

NO 9 Use soy or rice milk. These work great! and are the easiest of all to use and substitute. Be sure to get soy milk that is PLAIN, no honey or vanilla or any flavoring. Flavored (sweetened) milk works good in desserts or breads for baking, but can ruin gravy or soup.

FROGMORE GUMBO

You can't say you've been to the Deep South until you've tasted Gumbo. It's another of those recipes that everybody has their own special way of doing it, unchanged for 10 or so generations. I bet blood has been drawn over when to add the filé.

I add tofu and tempeh instead of shrimp or sausage. It's always a bit different and always delicious!!!

1/2 to 3/4 cup oil (make at least a couple
TBS. of this dark sesame oil)
1/2 to 3/4 cup flour
6 or 7 cups liquid (use whatever kind
you like)
5 or 6 ribs of celery, with leaves chopped up
1 large onion, chopped
1 bunch green onions, chopped
1 green pepper, chopped
1 red pepper, chopped
3 cloves garlic, mashed and chopped
1 to 2 lbs. okra, sliced
about 6 tomatoes, chopped
2 TBS. tamari or pick-a-peppa or a little of both
several good shakes of hot sauce
2 bay leaves
2 tsp. thyme
1 tsp. paprika
1 block tofu, cubed on the small side
1 steaming platter of rice
salt to taste

Gumbo Filé (optional...read about file at end of recipe)

Okay, so you're ready to start. Get a dutch oven or a big soup pot. I usually use my cast iron dutch oven. Heat the oil over low heat, when it's hot add the flour. This is supposed to cook over low heat for about 10- to 15 minutes until (this is the big secret) it's the color of a "copper penny." Now, add chopped onions, green onions, peppers, celery, thyme, and garlic. After this has sort of gotten going, add the chopped tofu and tempeh. Cook this over low heat for about 30 to 45 more minutes. It will be fairly dry; stir occasionally. Try not to add any more oil but if you have to, do.

Saute the okra in a separate skillet. When it's done add to pot along with water, tomatoes, parsley, bay leaves, pick-a-peppa, hot sauce, paprika, salt, and whatever else still needs to go in. Let it come to a boil, stir when you think of it. After an hour or so, taste and add more salt or a pinch of cayenne.

Serve this with a big platter of hot rice and pass the filé. The key to this recipe is low heat and almost constant stirring the first 45 minutes or so.

A NOTE ABOUT FILÉ

Filé is made out of ground sassafras leaves. It adds a flavor all it's own and if you can find it, please try it. If you add it directly to the pot, don't allow the soup to return to a boil or even cook much longer or the filé will make the gumbo stringy and not fit to eat. In many families the filé is passed around the table and each person suits himself.

It was the Choctaw Indians who first made filé. They called it "kombo" which is where we got gumbo from.

GAZPACHO

4 or 5 large, ripe tomatoes
1 or 2 cucumbers
1 or 2 bell peppers
1/4 cup lemon or lime juice
1/3 cup olive oil
1/2 cup green onion, chopped
3 or 4 ears corn
1/4 tsp. cayenne pepper
1/4 to 1/2 cup fresh jalepeno (if you like it hot)
2 avocados
1 or 2 TBS. honey
2 cloves garlic
pinch of dill
1/2 tsp. basil
1/2 tsp. paprika
a few sprigs of fresh parsley
salt
ice cubes
croutons

Mix in a blender the tomatoes, half the cucumber and peppers, lemon juice, olive oil, salt, cayenne, dill, basil, garlic, and honey until smooth.

Chop the rest of the cucumber and peppers, jalepeno, avocado, corn (cut right off the cobb and barely cooked), and chopped onions. Add to the soup and let chill a few hours. Before serving add a few cracked ice cubes to each bowl. A side dish of croutons makes Gazpacho perfect for an August lunch.

P.S. This is another recipe that I stand and taste as I stir it up. It usually takes a few more sprinkles of this or that before it tastes right (and it's always a different amount of this or that.) I guess it just depends on your mood. Anyway, while tasting, remember it should have a bit of a kick to it, and all the flavors will come out more after it sits awhile.

Palumbo's Provincetown Mushroom-Barley Soup

1/2 cup barley
3 1/2 pints soup stock or water
1 onion, chopped
3 carrots
4 TBS. celery, chopped
1/2 cup mushrooms
4 TBS. butter or margarine
1 tsp. salt
1/2 tsp. pepper
4 TBS. sour cream or 4 TBS. tofu blended with 1/2 cup soup stock or fake sour cream

Simmer the barley in 1/2 the liquid. In the rest of the liquid cook the onion, carrots, celery, and mushrooms until they're all tender. Now, combine the cooked barley with the vegetables and add butter, salt, and pepper. Remove from heat and stir in sour cream or tofu mixture.

Fix this for someone you can cuddle up to and give them lots of kisses on the cheek. That's the way Palumbo said you have to do it. Palumbo also says that she uses sour cream and that if you like your soup really rich, to go on and use the whole container of sour cream; she often does!

MISO SOUP

This is another one of my main staples. When I live in a cold climate I eat this for breakfast. It can be made with any vegetables you like, not just the ones I name. It's even good with just onions, like french onion soup. When I'm sick or just plain weary and weak, a bowl of miso soup revives me faster than anything. It has that real grandmotherly feel to it. Miso is also a good base for any soup or beans. There are all kinds of miso from rice to barley, red to yellow to brown. Some are sweet and some are on the sour side; they're all delicious. There is a live enzyme in miso, like in yogurt. To keep it alive don't let your soup come to a boil after adding it. I even like miso spread on toast with butter. Start looking for it in health food stores, and oriental stores. Some supermarkets have it in the Chinese or Japanese sections.

1 onion, chopped in crescents and pieces
2 carrots, chopped in small pieces
1 clove garlic, smashed and chopped
1/2 cabbage, sliced thin
any green (kale, collards, parsley, water cress)
1 handful rice or 1/4 to 1/2 package of favorite noodle (I like ribbons, or any skinny noodles)
3 TBS. sesame oil or safflower
1/4 to 1/2 cup wakame or arame

Heat oil in pot, add onions, garlic, carrots, cabbage, or any other veggie you're using. If you are using seaweed which is completely optional, put it in enough water to cover it and let sit about 10 minutes. After the wakame has soaked add it to the rest of the vegetables. Continue cooking about 10 more minutes. Add about 6 cups water and let simmer until vegetables are done. Dip out about 1 cup of the broth, and dissolve 1/4 to 1/2 cup of miso in it. When completely dissolved, add back to soup. Put on low heat, don't let it return to a boil. Serve in about 10 to 15 minutes.

As a garnish use finely chopped green onion, or parsley. Sesame seeds are also good. If you want also, add a few small cubes of tofu or a handful of sprouts at the end of cooking time with the miso.

About adding the rice or noodles... it can be left over, already cooked, put in towards the end of cooking time. If not cooked, fine, add either uncooked rice or noodles more towards the beginning of the process. When the rice or noodles are done, then it's time to put in the miso.

The fast and easy way to do this is put big spoon full of miso in a teacup and pour almost boiling over it. let sit 5 minutes, stir and it's ready. This is good if you are sick and don't feel like making a whole soup.

There are a million versions of this soup; it doesn't matter which one you try, just as long as you try it!

Back Roads Lentil Soup

1 onion, diced
1 carrot, chopped into matchsticks
3 cloves garlic, smashed
1 or 2 cups dry lentils (about twice to 3 times as much as much water)
1 bunch spinach (about 1 lb.) or other similar green such as kale or chard
2 bay leaves
1 TBS. per serving of rice vinegar
salt, pepper, tamari to taste

Add onion, carrot, garlic to hot oil. Saute until soft and turning brown. Add the tamari, lentils, and water. Give it a stir and throw in the bay leaves. Let it all come to a boil and turn down to a simmer. When the lentils are getting soft add the spinach leaves and cover so they can wilt. Stir while adding salt, pepper, and tamari. Feel free to add water if you want a thinner soup. When the spinach is wilted the soup is done.

(Vinegar can be added to the pot or put on the table for your guests to serve themselves. It brings out the taste of the lentils like nobody's business.) Whoever gets the big leaf gets a kiss.

BROCCOLI CHEDDAR

1 large bunch broccoli
1 stick butter or margarine
1/3 cup flour
1 to 1 1/2 quarts milk or soymilk (always be sure to use plain, the kind with vanilla and honey won't work)
1/2 to 3/4 lb. extra sharp cheddar cheese (or you can mix in nutritional yeast cheese) or fake cheddar

Cut up broccoli and put in heavy pot with butter. Let saute with lid on. Stir in flour, let brown. The broccoli should be getting pretty soft by now. Add milk or soymilk and grated cheese. Cook on low heat until thick and very smooth. Stir every once and a while. Add salt and pepper. It's not a long time cooking. This soup is always a winner. Make a bread or muffin to go with it if you have time. If not, toast will complete it.

Marge's secret: if your soup "breaks" (cooks too quickly on a burner that's too hot and starts to become curds and whey) put the whole shebang into the blender and call it bisque.

POTATO SOUP

6 to 8 red skinned potatoes
1 stick butter or margarine
1 to 1 1/2 quarts milk or soymilk (warm)
salt and pepper
1/2 cup or so of fresh parsley, chopped

The king of comfort foods...it's so cheap and so easy...is that why it tastes so good? Here's how I do it:

Cook potatoes (these can be leftovers or cooked in advance). Pour off most of the water, then mash. By mash, I mean add the butter and about 1/2 the warm milk. Begin mashing with a potato masher but don't feel you're supposed to get all the lumps out. Add the rest of the milk and simmer over low heat until heated through. Add parsley now. You can also add 1 tsp. of dill weed or 1 tsp. caraway seeds to the soup. Chopped green onion is a great garnish. Serve this soup at once and plan to eat it all...it looses something by the next day. Be careful not to overcook!

Croutons

1/4 stick margarine
1 clove garlic, smashed and chopped
(or 1/2 tsp. garlic powder)
1 TBS. chives, chopped
1 tsp. kelp powder
1 tsp. sage
1 tsp. thyme
1 TBS. poppy seed
1 tsp. salt
2 tsp. oregano
5 or 6 slices leftover bread

This will make quite a bit, but it keeps well and they're great munchies...

Melt butter in a small sauce pan. Add herbs and spices, let simmer a few minutes and remove from heat.

Spread the bread slices out on the table or counter. Spoon a little of the herb butter mixture onto each piece and spread around with the back of the spoon. Stack all the slices on top of one another with the top one butter side down. Slice the whole pile into cubes. Spread the cubes on a cookie sheet and bake at 350^ for 20 minutes, or until toasted, tossing them once or twice to get them evenly browned.

These smell so good that everyone in the house will come in the kitchen to ask, "What are you making?"

Put the croutons in a big bowl and serve. If you like cheese, sprinkle on some parmesan while the croutons are hot and toss lightly. The heat will make the cheese stick. Add good tasting nutritional yeast also if you like.

DUMPLINGS

1 cup flour, whole wheat is fine
1/4 cup wheat germ (if you have it)
3 tsp. baking powder
1/2 tsp. salt
1 TBS. honey
2 portions egg replacer
1/2 cup cold water

This is the complete recipe. At this point you may also add 1/4 to 1/2 cup chopped parsley, chopped onion, nutritional yeast, or grated cheese.

Mix the dry ingredients in a bowl, make a well and add the rest. Just barely stir till the dough leaves the sides of the bowl. These dumplings are made with thick soups (split pea, vegetable, lentil, or noodle). Take a clean spoon and place a spoonful of batter onto the soup. Be sure the soup is steaming hot when you do this (not necessarily rapidly boiling, but hot enough to start cooking the dumplings right away). Continue spooning batter over top of soup until covered. Make sure the lid fits tight. You can invert a glass pie plate over the pot and watch them cook. Remember to leave the lid on—don't keep taking it off to see what's happening. It's the steam that cooks the dumplings.

Dumplings can also be cooked on top of pieces of simmering tofu in a skillet. Just make sure the lid fits tight and the tofu is juicy.

These dumplings won't get tough because they don't have eggs in them. Check the dumplings after about 10 to 12 minutes. You can prick them with a fork to make sure they're done in the middle.

TOMATO SAUCE

 EFTOVERS

Burgers And Special Sauce

Uncreamed Spinach On Toast

Brown Rice Muffins

Oatmeal Molasses Muffins

J.J. Gettes Fried Noodles

Fried Rice

"MEN ARE USUALLY MORE CARE-
FUL OF THE BREED OF THEIR
HORSES AND DOGS THAN OF
THEIR CHILDREN."
WILLIAM PENN 1644-1718

"GET ALL THE GOOD YOU CAN
OUTTA SEVENTEEN, CAUSE IT
SURE WEARS OUT IN ONE HELL
OF A HURRY."
PAUL NEWMAN AS HUD

BURGERS

The best thing to make with leftovers is burgers. At the end of the week, when my fridge is full of little bowls, each with 2 spoonfuls of something different, or those beans that I'm sick of moving from shelf to shelf (that weren't very good in the first place), that's when I make burgers. I have never been able to come up with a pat recipe for this because I always have different things in my fridge. But here's how I do it, step by step.
I have used all of the following in my recipe, and they have all turned out great. Try to have something fairly substantial as the basis for the mix. Any grain will work as a main ingredient, the older the better.

LEFTOVER	SPAGHETTI
MILLET	BLACK-EYED PEAS
COUS-COUS	MASHED POTATOES
CHICK PEAS	BOILED OR BAKED SQUASH
ADUKI BEANS	BREAD CRUMBS
LENTILS	POTATO SOUP
DAHL	ANY KIND OF BEANS

Any kind of soup or sauce will come in handy now. You are going to have to make all this stick together somehow, aren't you? So look in your fridge for something that will work. Puree any kind of soup and pour that in. Some tamari, a little sherry, whatever.

MISO SOUP	SPLIT PEA SOUP
LENTIL SOUP	VEGETARIAN CHILI

Now remember that bowl of oatmeal that sat out all morning and then someone put it in the fridge? Get it out and toss it in. Left over cereals are perfect for a burger mix.

RICE CREAM	7 GRAIN CEREAL
OATMEAL	TOASTED SEEDS OR NUTS
BARLEY	HUMMUS
GRATED CARROTS OR ZUCCHINI	
ONIONS OR PEPPERS, CHOPPED FINE	

So now you have an idea what to make the mix out of. Roll up your sleeves and start working it with your hands. Continue working and mashing with your hands and fingers until it is well mixed. Try to determine for yourself what kind of consistency you have. Will it form a patty? If it's too mushy add wheat germ or any kind of flour. This will make it sticky and firm. Nutritional yeast also works really well, or milk powder if you like to use that. Stir this around till you have the consistency you want. Now coat both sides with flour, nutritional yeast or sesame seeds and fry in a hot skillet until crispy brown on both sides. Don't fiddle around with these too much while they're cooking (pushing them around with a spatula, etc.), as they do best when left alone. These burgers can also be baked. Serve with the works, including the "Special Sauce" for those die-hard Big Mac memories.

SPECIAL SAUCE

1 TBS. honey
1 cup mayonnaise
1 tsp. grated onion
1/4 cup relish
2 TBS. ketchup

Mix this together well and enjoy on your burger or reuben anytime...

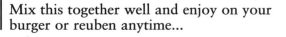

UNCREAMED SPINACH on TOAST

When I was a little girl in grade school, I used to walk home for lunch everyday. This was not an ordinary walk. There was a little path that wound around through the woods and a little creek. If you were a good jumper (and it hadn't been raining too much), you could hop from rock to rock, all the way down the creek. We used to swing off a grape vine that put Cheetah to shame. If you didn't drop off at the right time, you'd slam into a wall of rocks and poison ivy.

It was a great place to play before and after school, but on my way home for lunch I was usually alone. One day in the late spring, the water in the creek had gotten warm enough to wade in, and I had my shoes off just fooling around in the creek meandering home. I thought the world was my big red apple. About that time, I looked down and right under my foot was a huge black snake. He was just stetched out, smack-dab in the middle of the path, baking in the sun. That snake took off like greased lightin' and so did I. I don't remember my feet touching the ground until I was standing in the kitchen telling my mamma about it, and helping her fix lunch. This is what we made...

Find at least 1/4 to 1/2 cup of some leftover vegetable.

WE USED ANY OF THESE:

cauliflower	watercress	peas
mushrooms	yellow squash	corn
asparagus	artichokes	kale
zucchini	broccoli	spinach
tofu, cubed	crumbled tempeh	

If you don't have any of these things left over, most of these vegetables are fast cooking and will work fresh. You just need to give the greens time to wilt, or the vegetables time to get soft.

2 or 3 TBS. margarine
1/4 cup flour (rice or millet flour is nice)
1 cup soy milk, vegetable broth, or water

Melt the margarine in a skillet. Add the flour and stir around a few minutes, then put in the spinach or whatever vegetable you're using. Remember, if this has already been cooked once, it won't need to cook much. Stir around till well mixed and add the liquid. Stir until thickened and spoon overtoast. Of course, you can add chopped onions, parsley, mustard, nuts, and lots of different things to this recipe, but just plain, it's still my favorite lunch.

BROWN RICE MUFFINS

1 1/4 cup whole wheat flour
2 tsp. baking powder
1/2 tsp. salt
2 TBS. honey
2 eggs or egg replacer
1 cup soy or dairy milk (or water)
1/4 cup oil or melted margarine
1 cup cold cooked brown rice

Stir the dry ingredients together. In another bowl, combine the eggs, liquid, honey, oil, and rice. Add to the flour mixture and stir just till moist. Pour into greased muffin tin and bake at 425^ for about 20 minutes or till done. These are delicious muffins. I like to make them for breakfast out of last night's rice.

OATMEAL MOLASSES MUFFINS

It never fails, after breakfast is all eaten and done, you're cleaning up the dishes and start to wash the oatmeal pot, and there is just a little bit left in the bottom. It's cold now, and nobody's hungry anyway. Still, there's something in me that balks at scraping this into the garbage. I let it sit in the fridge till it looks like a science project and then I scrape it into the garbage.

This is the recipe that forever puts an end to the yucky oatmeal saga.

2 cups whole wheat flour
almost 1/2 cup molasses (just a little less)
1 tsp. baking powder
pinch of cinnamon and ginger
1/2 tsp. salt
1 to 1 1/2 cup leftover oatmeal
1/2 cup water
1/4 cup oil
2 eggs or replacer
1/2 cup pecan or any nut, chopped

Sift the dry ingredients together including the spices and salt. Mash together oatmeal, water, molasses, oil, and egg replacer. Stir until just moist. When smooth, add to the dry ingredients and stir just till moist. Then stir in the oatmeal and nuts. Spoon into greased muffin tins and bake at 400^ for 20 minutes. These muffins are scrumptious.

J.J. Gettes Fried Noodles

approx. 5 cups any kind of leftover noodles
green onion, sliced lengthwise
3 stalks broccoli, cauliflower, summer squash,
or cabbage
1 cup chopped mushrooms (optional)
1 red pepper, sliced into long skinny strips
tamari
several cloves garlic, minced
salt and pepper
olive or sesame oil
You can omit all the veggies if you want and
just use noodles, oil and garlic

Why is it so easy to make too much pasta? I don't know about you, but I always enthusiastically dump in at least twice as much as I need, and it sits in the refrigerator for a week before I throw it out. This is one of the ways to make leftovers taste better than it did originally. If you want, cook it a little longer let the noodles get crispy.

Heat the oil in a wok or skillet and when it's hot, throw in the garlic, ginger and broccoli. A few minutes later, the pepper. When the broccoli turns bright green, you'll notice. Put in the noodles and green onion. Barely toss and add tamari, salt, pepper, and a little more oil if you need it. Don't stir this, but gently toss, and when the noodles are well heated and you can smell the ginger cooking, then it's done.

Do you know the best way to prepare broccoli? I had always heard this and I thought it was a waste of time until I tried it. Cut off the very rough end, cut little slashes in the base of the stem, pull each "slash" down with a little jerk and the tough part will tear right off. The part of the stem that's left is so tender and sweet, it makes the stalk as good as the flower.

FRIED RICE

2 to 3 cups leftover rice
2 or 3 of your favorite vegetables (any will
work fine: onions, green onions, snow peas,
broccoli, celery, spinach, brussel sprouts,
cabbage, cauliflower, sprouts, mushrooms)
3 or 4 TBS. oil
tamari to taste

The secret of fried rice is that it has to be made out of rice that is at least one day old. If you try to make this out of fresh hot rice, it will get all gooey and stick together. Heat the oil in a skillet or wok and when it's hot, add vegetables starting with the heaviest and working down to the lightest ones. Don't use more than 3 different kinds, as it will get too crazy. When vegies are just tender, add the rice and stir quickly. If you are using sprouts, add them now, then the tamari. When rice is heated through, it is ready to serve. Some people like their rice with egg in it. I don't, but if you do want it, scrape all the food away from a little spot in the middle of the skillet. Add a tad of oil and when it's very hot, break the egg into the cleared spot. Scramble it very quickly. When done stir into the rest of the rice. Don't just have this with Chinese food. It's good enough to have any time, even for breakfast.

COOKING OUTDOORS

"FIRE IS THE
BEST OF SERVANTS;
BUT WHAT A MASTER!"
THOMAS CARLYLE 1795-1881

"THERE IS SOMETHING IN
OCTOBER SETS THE GYPSY
BLOOD ASTIR."
ELISS CARMAN 1861-1929

"ALL THE MODERN
INCONVENIENCES..."
MARK TWAIN 1835-1910

Things ⏢ Remember When You're Cooking Out

IN THE BACKYARD:

No1 Have a good, dependable grill or hibachi. You can make a nice grill out of a medium sized oil drum. Make sure of the source so it's non-toxic. Place 2 cinder blocks on either side to sturdy it, and cover with your own rack. I've done this myself and it works quite well.

No2 Don't forget the brickettes, lighter fluid, or matches.

No3 Try to have a small table beside the grill to keep food and utensils on. You never know when you could step back right onto a butcher knife or right into the middle of the main course.

No4 Have several good, dependable pot holders on hand.

No5 Try to have some bug spray around.

No6 Most importantly, keep it simple—you don't need all kinds of nutty gadgets around; they will just make everyone nervous and get in the way.

No7 Have a couple of adaptable, long-handled utensils to use around the grill, also a pastry brush. Don't use plastic or wooden handles

No8 Don't hog the grill all to yourself. Men and young teenage boys love to play with fire. Let everyone have a chance to play.

IN THE WOODS:

№ 1 Most importantly, don't forget the matches.

№ 2 Don't build a fire under a tree; the flames could jump up and catch the branches on fire.

№ 3 Build your fire in a clear space with big rocks around it.

№ 4 Bury your trash that can't be burned.

№ 5 Again, keep it simple. Just bring what you'll really need. The wild doesn't need a lot of red tape.

№ 6 Don't forget: a bottle or can opener, a good knife, a potholder(s), and a good skillet or pot.

№ 7 Don't feel bad if something burns; even black and crusty food cooked out tastes better, and besides, charcoal is good for the digestive system.

№ 8 Don't use utensils that have plastic or wooden handles because they can melt and catch fire easily.

№ 9 Wander around your campsite and pick up different sizes of wood; get tiny pieces, some middle sized ones, and a couple of giant sized ones. Do this first, while it's still light out; you'll never find any wood in the dark.

№ 10 Don't get green wood—it won't burn. Try to break it over your knee; if it doesn't just crack in two then it's green.

№ 11 Remember, fire represents the sign of Leo on this earth. Like the lion, it thrives on attention. Think about your Leo friends, when given the proper attention they burn brilliantly. If not, they'll go into another room and sulk. It's the same with your campfire. Respect it, give it energy, and watch it burn! Ignore it, and it will run away from you or worse, go out, just to get your attention.

BAKED BEANS

3 or 4 cups dried white, pinto, or lima beans
1/2 cup molasses
2 onions, sliced
1/4 cup prepared mustard
3 TBS. miso dissolved in
1/2 cup bean cooking water
1 or 2 TBS. grated ginger
salt and pepper
pinch allspice
1 TBS. brown sugar

Soak beans in water overnight. Rinse and cook with enough water to cover for about 2 hours or until done. Pour off 1/2 the water and mix in the other ingredients. Turn into a deep dish casserole, arrange onions on top, and bake in a 350^ oven for 1 hour. This is a delicious recipe and very spicy. It's a good one for any backyard picnic. Of course, this can cook in a pot over a fire, or in the coals of your own fireplace.

SENTER'S WAY

My brother spends more time out fooling around in the woods than just about anybody. He would rather spend the night in the deep woods or in a tee-pee than anything else you could think of. It wasn't easy to get him to sit down and write anything but here's what he had to say about it:

You must have an indestructible pot of some sort. None works better than a deep dish cast iron skillet with removable lid. (Lids keep out ashes and falling leaves). This may prove to be a might bit heavy if back-packing a distance but they come in all sizes. Whatever you use, it must have a good fitting lid and contain no burnable parts (plastic handles, wooden knobs or handles, etc.) as all these items will invariably go up in smoke on an open fire.

Remember to take a thick potholder with you; open fires tend to get very hot. Start fire at least 30 minutes before you are ready to cook a meal. Line the outside of your fire with big flat rocks—they'll work good as counter space when you need to pull something off the fire or turn it down to "low" so to speak. Burn lots of small dry sticks first so you can begin accumulating a large bed of coals. A hot bed of coals several inches thick is what you want to cook on...not a roaring fire.

After you have an acceptable amount of hot coals, put in two or three bigger sticks as big around as your fist. Place them crosswise onto the fire. This will provide you with something fairly flat and steady to set your pans on.

If the fire is built into a dug out hole, 1/2 foot deep, and surrounded by another 1/2 foot of table rocks, you'll be a lot less likely to succumb to the swirling of wood smoke, chasing you around the fire all night. You can cut down the draft and that helps the smoke rise straight up.

Don't forget a big sharp knife, stirring spoon, can opener, and matches.

In the middle of nowhere I like to wash my dishes in a creek or river. No soap or washcloth is needed, no brillo pad. Find a nice sandy spot at the edge of the water that has a lot of pebbles. Scoop up a handful of sand and pebbles and put into your pan or skillet. Use the abrasiveness of the grit to be your kind of steel wool. Clean creek water is essential for this. If in doubt, just use soap and water.

Shish-Ke-Bobs

This recipe will forever put to rest the idea that "vegetarians can't cook out." This is a great thing to have when you are having friends over to eat. People just can't help but get caught up in some phase of shish-ke-bobbing—lighting the fire, sticking the vegetables on the skewers, or moving them around on the grill. I'm always surprised at how someone I'd never suspect, comes right over and picks up a big fork or pot holder and gets completely into it.

Here is what you'll need: enough skewers for everyone. You can use coat hangers but they tend to get pretty funky. Most butchers at the supermarket have small wooden skewers around, or check the oriental market, they usually have long skewers around just for this reason.

Of course, there are many vegetables and things to put on your ke-bob.

HERE'S WHAT I HAVE USED:

firm marinated tofu
soysages
brussel sprouts
steamed or fried tempeh
tomatoes (quartered works best)
green and red peppers
yellow squash
chunks baby corn
artichoke hearts
giant mushrooms
quartered red onions
cubed eggplant
whole okra
whole garlic clove

Usually I make up 6 or 7 shish-ke-bobs to get people inspired to do their own. Have everything set up on a table, in little bowls or saucers, etc., and let big appetites take over from there.

BARBECUE "CHICKEN" TEMPEH

2 or 3 blocks of tempeh steamed (20 minutes)
1 onion, chopped
a few TBS. oil
about 5 cups of White Woman's barbecue sauce

When the coals are ready (you don't want them too hot) coat tempeh generously on both sides with sauce and lay gently over the coals. Brush on more sauce as the tempeh grills.

The tempeh should be cut into quarters, big enough so that the pieces can't fall through the grill. Cut some in half, width-wise, if you don't like it too thick.

Marinated ⁓Grilled⁓ Vegetables

zucchini	yellow summer squash
carrots	broccoli
cauliflower	eggplant
tomato halves	quartered red peppers

Make a marinade out of one of the recipes that follow, or look in the chapter on salad dressings and find one you like better. Slice the vegetables, making them as long as possible so they won't fall through the grill later. Cut the carrots, yellow squash, eggplant, and zucchini lengthwise. Cut the broccoli into spears and the cauliflower into fat flowerettes. Let these marinate for 3 to 4 hours. Toss them when you think of it. Lay these over a medium grill or put in a grill basket for about 10 minutes, or till roasted, brown and tender.

Marinades

NO. 1

1/4 cup tamari
1/4 cup dark sesame oil
2 TBS. balsamic vinegar
1/2 cup dry white wine
1/4 cup sesame oil
2 cloves garlic, smashed
1 TBS. Grey Poupon

NO. 2

1/4 cup tamari
1/4 cup water
2 or 3 cloves garlic, smashed
1/2 TBS. grated ginger

NO. 3

1/2 cup olive oil
1/4 cup lime juice
2 TBS. honey

GRILLED TEMPEH

Usually if I am cooking out, I'll go ahead and do a couple of different things. Here's a good way to do tempeh or tofu:

2 to 3 blocks tempeh or tofu,
sliced and marinated in:
1 cup tamari mixed with 1 cup water
1 TBS. dry mustard
2 cloves garlic, smashed
1/4 cup bourbon
3 TBS. molasses

Lightly saute the tempeh or tofu first in a little oil and tamari, then marinate for about 2 hours. Lay over hot coals, keep basting, and turn when necessary. This should be finished, with a nice flavor, in 5 to 8 minutes.

Carrot*Dogs

If you have never taken advantage of this alternative then please do so. Carrot dogs are real easy and they are a good, cheap food to cook out. They don't crumble and fall in the fire, and even burned they taste great.

8 to 10 medium sized carrots

GLAZE:
2 to 3 TBS. honey
1 tsp. grated ginger
1/2 stick margarine
1 TBS. tamari
(You can also use barbecue sauce
if you have some)

Cut the end of each carrot. If it's a big fat one cut it in half. Steam the carrots lightly until they are soft or until about 3/4 done.

Combine glaze ingredients in small, heated sauce pan. When melted, remove from heat.

If you are cooking outdoors lay carrots on the grill and brush with glaze, barbecue sauce, or whatever marinade you choose. Turn occasionally and brush when needed. When these are golden (it won't be easy to tell since they're already orange) they're done. Just use your nose.

You can also wrap these in aluminum foil and cook in your fireplace, or put on a cookie sheet and put under the broiler in the oven.

Put these in buns and have all the trimmings ready. Chili, onions, relish, mustard, tomatoes, sauerkraut.

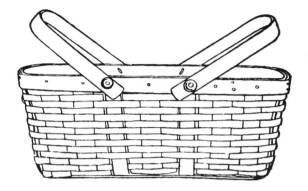

GRILLED RED ONIONS AND GARLIC

5 or 6 red onions, vidalia, or what you have
1 or 2 whole bulb's garlic

Marinate the onions in your favorite marinade, or:

1/4 to 1/2 cup olive oil
3 TBS. tamari
1 TBS. lemon juice
salt and pepper

Cut the onions into halves - do not peel. Dredge cut half in olive oil. Put cut side down over coals. They will take at least 30 minutes. These can cook forever and still be great. I think slightly burned tastes best. To eat, use onion tassel as handles, peel back skin and bite in. Garlic. Cut entire bulb in half, dredge in oil and grill along with onion. The garlic won't take as long to cook as the onion. Put these directly over hot coals and turn when necessary. You may want to run a toothpick through these because as they cook, they soften and may fall through the grill.

POCKETBOOK STEW

The easiest things are always the best. I like to make this when kids are around; it's so easy they can do it by themselves. Also, this is a great fireplace dinner. One night we made a bunch of these little "pockets" and a few of them got lost back in the coals. When I poked up the fire the next morning, I found them, still warm...boy what a breakfast...

These can be cooked anywhere on the outdoor grill or on the coals of a campfire. They're virtually impossible to ruin, and like most things you cook over a fire, they even taste good burnt.

1 block tofu or tempeh, marinated and sliced (This is completely optional but it's really good and makes it more of a "meal")
3 to 5 potatoes, sliced
2 to 3 onions, sliced
4 to 5 carrots, sliced in sticks
(Remember with your vegetables the thinner you slice them, the faster they'll cook)
margarine
salt and pepper
aluminum foil, torn in 9 by 9 inch pieces

Lay the foil down on the table, sunny side up. Lay a piece of tofu or tempeh on, along with 3 or 4 slices of potato, a few slices of onion, 2 or 3 carrot sticks, salt and pepper, and top with a pat of margarine. Roll up the sides of the foil. Try to make it real tight all over so the juice doesn't all run out when it starts to cook. Place on medium coals. Check after about 30 minutes depending on the size of the fire.

When you have finished wrapping everything up, if you have any one item leftover (onions, carrots, potatoes) just wrap it up and add a pinch of salt, pepper, and margarine and put it on the coals to cook. These usually end up being the surprise hit of the night.

If there is an origin for this recipe, it must be the Girl Scouts, as it's the first thing any scout ever cooks out. I remember helping a group of 10 year olds get their Outdoor Cooking Merit Badge. After the whole ordeal was over we were sitting around gnawing burnt marshmallows off sticks. I asked one little girl if she remembered the name of what we had for dinner. She had a confused look on her face and said, "I think it was called Pocketbook Stew." Close, but no cigar.

Roasted Corn

10 ears of corn with the husks still on

Pull back the tops of the husks and remove the silk. Put the husks back up and soak in salted water for 5 minutes. Grill over hot coals for about 10 to 15 minutes. Turn these frequently. You may find that your grill is filled up with burgers and shish-ke-bobs and there is no room for the corn; don't worry, you can pile it in your oven and roast it for 20 to 25 minutes at 400^.

City "Chicken" Legs

2 blocks tofu
1 cup bread crumbs
1/2 cup good tasting nutritional yeast
1/2 cup wheat germ or oatmeal
1 tsp. thyme
1/2 cup onion, chopped fine
1/2 cup parsley, chopped
2 TBS. tamari
10 skewers

In a bowl, mix all the ingredients together. Work this all together really good with your hands. It should hold together easily.

Gently, but firmly, press a good bit of tofu mixture around 1/2 of the skewer. You may want to rub your hands with oil before you start, as this will make it easier to handle.

If you're cooking these outdoors, brush generously with White Woman Barbecue Sauce, or with a bit of melted margarine or oil. Place each one over the coals, turning and basting them whenever necessary.

If you're cooking these indoors, then of course, you can do the tofu legs with barbecue sauce and bake them in your oven. If you don't want to do that, then do this: cover the bottom of a heavy skillet with oil. Roll the legs in flour (chickpea, sesame, or whole wheat). Place gently in hot oil, fry till crispy on all sides.

Don't use not being able to find skewers as an excuse to not make these; you can always use empty popsicle sticks. Most oriental markets carry a good selection of skewers.

BREADS

Kitty Sue's Cinnamon Coconut Rolls

Blue Ribbon Blueberry Muffins

Hoecakes

Sarah's Prize Winners

Buttermilk Biscuits

Granny's Banana Bread

Hushpuppies

Bobby Sand's Scones

Flour Tortillas

Shady Side Nut Muffins

Coffee Ridge Pineapple Nut Bread

Rocky Fork Drop Biscuits

Short'nin Bread

Mamma's Famous Cheese Bread

Buns

Easy Overnight Cinnamon Rolls

Mom's Dining Room Refrigerator Rolls

Izzie Cohen's Bagels

English Muffins

Properly Made Tea

"THERE IS NO SPECTACLE ON EARTH MORE APPEALING THAN THAT OF A WOMAN IN THE ACT OF COOKING DINNER FOR SOMEONE SHE LOVES."
THOMAS WOLFE 1900-1938

"I NEVER HAD
A PIECE OF TOAST
PARTICULARLY LONG AND WIDE,
BUT FELL UPON
THE SANDED FLOOR,
AND ALWAYS ON
THE BUTTERED SIDE."
JAMES PAYNE 1830-1898

Kitty Sue's Cinnamon Coconut Rolls

This is a wonderful recipe, because no matter what kind of cook you are, or what time of the day or night it is, you'll probably have these ingredients sitting around your kitchen.

TOPPING:
3/4 cup brown sugar
1/4 cup butter or margarine
2/3 cup coconut
dash of cinnamon

1 3/4 cup plus 2 TBS. flour
2 tsp. baking powder
1/2 tsp. salt
3/4 cup milk or soymilk
1/4 cup margarine

Cut butter into the dry ingredients until the size of peas. Add milk slowly until moist. Turn out and knead for 20 seconds. Pat dough into a rectangle. Spread the coconut mixture in the bottom of the cooking pan and place (piece if you have to) the dough over the top. Place in pan and bake at 425^ for about 20 minutes or until done. Remove from the oven cut in squares. Lift out with spatula and serve up-side down on serving plate. You'll feel just like Betty Crocker. Remove all from pan now or it will stick and you'll be a shamed Betty Crocker.

Blue Ribbon Blueberry Muffins

1/4 cup soft margarine
1/2 cup honey
1 egg
3/4 cup milk or soymilk
1/4 tsp. vanilla
1 3/4 cups flour (white or whole wheat)
2 1/2 tsp. baking powder
1/2 tsp. salt
1 cup blueberries

Preheat oven to 425^. In a medium bowl, cream the margarine and honey. Beat in egg, milk, and vanilla. In a small bowl, stir together flour, baking powder, and salt. Add to wet mixture and stir. The combined mixture will be moist and a little lumpy. Mix about a TBS. of flour with the berries and fold into batter. Spoon into greased muffin tins and bake at 425^ for 25 minutes or until evenly golden brown.

HOECAKES

Hoecakes as made at the "Big House:"

2 cups flour
1 cup milk
1 teaspoon yeast
2 TBS. butter

Mix ingredients well and kneed. Roll out with rolling pin, cut criss-cross with a knife, like diamonds, and bake in oven.

Hoecakes as made in the "Cabin:"

1 tsp. lard
2 cups flour
1 tsp. salt
boiling water to make batter

"These cakes may be baked on a griddle, just as you would a griddle cake, and served with butter. But the old Southern cooks always baked them on a hoe on hot coals in front of the fire out in the open air, just before their cabin doors, or in their cabin before a roaring fire. Hence the name "Hoecake." The term hoecake, so extensively used by the field hands, was taken up by masters and mistresses and applied to the biscuit bread described above."

Picayune Creole Cookbook 1901
I got this recipe from one of my favorite cookbooks, "River Road Recipes." It is one of those regional cookbooks put out by a women's group that's full of things one couldn't live without such as "Salad for 70." The whole recipe is 18 heads of lettuce and 8 bunches of parsley. It's a great book though and will provide hours of entertainment.

SARAH'S PRIZE WINNERS

1 1/4 buttermilk, sourmilk, or soymilk
1 cup whole bran
1/4 cup margarine
1/3 cup honey
1 egg or replacer
1 1/2 cup whole wheat flour
1 1/2 tsp. baking powder
1/2 tsp. salt
1/4 tsp. baking soda
1 cup grated cheddar cheese

Pour the buttermilk over the bran and let it sit until the mixture is soft. Cream the honey, margarine, and egg in a separate bowl. Mix the dry ingredients, then add the creamed mixture alternately with the milk-bran mixture. Stir in the grated cheese. Grease muffin tins and fill 2/3 full with batter. Bake in hot oven (400^) for about 30 minutes. My grandmother won first prize in a contest with this recipe. After you try them you'll know why.

BUTTERMILK BISCUITS

2 cups flour (use white or whole wheat in any combination; just remember, the lighter the flour, the lighter the biscuits)
1 TBS. honey
2 1/2 tsp. baking powder
1/2 tsp. salt
1/4 tsp. baking soda
about 3/4 cup buttermilk
5 TBS. melted margarine or butter

Preheat the oven to 450^ until it's nice and hot. Mix the dry ingredients in a bowl and make a well. Pour in the buttermilk, honey, and melted butter. **This is the tricky part.** Stir with as few strokes as possible, just until the dough follows the fork around the bowl. Too much stirring will make your biscuits like little rocks. Turn the batter out onto a floured board and knead gently about 6 times, just to help it take shape. Roll this out with a rolling pin, handling as little as possible, to about 1/4 to 1/2 inch thickness. Cut with a biscuit cutter, careful not to twist the cutter. Put these on a greased cookie sheet and bake 10 to 15 minutes.

GRANNY'S BANANA ∽BREAD∽

1/4 cup margarine
1/2 cup honey
3 eggs or egg replacer
3 mashed bananas (the riper, the better)
1/3 cup water mixed with 3 TBS. milk
1 tsp. vanilla
1 tsp. salt
2 tsp. baking powder
1 tsp. baking soda
2 cups flour (white or whole wheat or a combination)
1/4 cup wheat germ
1/2 cup raisans
3/4-1 cup walnuts or pecans

The secret of this recipe is to cream the wet ingredients as smoothly as possible. Use an electric mixer if you have one or even a processor. The smoother the batter, the lighter your bread will be, so get those ingredients mixed up real well. Mix the dry ingredients and with as few strokes as possible blend them into the banana honey mixture. Stir in the nuts and raisins. Pour the batter into a greased loaf pan. As this is a pretty heavy bread don't use a real deep pan, or your bread will never get done in the middle. Put it in small loaf pans and bake at 350^ for 1 hour, or until a straw comes out clean. This recipe also makes good muffins, so don't just cook it always as one long loaf.

Hushpuppies

2 cups cornmeal
1 tsp. baking powder
1/2 tsp. baking soda
1 egg or egg replacer
1 TBS. honey
1 cup buttermilk
dash of cayenne
1 tsp. salt
1/4 to 1/2 cup green onions, chopped fine
1/8 tsp. garlic powder
1 TBS. grated onion
enough oil (peanut is good) to deep fry

A dog's life is not so bad!

Mix the dry ingredients in a bowl and make a well. Stir the buttermilk, egg, and honey together and pour into the well. Stir and add the onions. Drop this mixture by spoonfuls into the hot oil (375^), and fry until golden. I like to make these with tempeh, frying both at the same time. Hushpuppies are a great change from cornbread and they go real well with vegetables.

How about boiled potatoes, collard greens, and hushpuppies for dinner tonight?

They are also as good with ketchup as they are with tartar sauce.

At any Southern outdoor to-do there are bound to be dogs and where there are dogs there most assuredly are a few puppies. The hounds would start; the pups would follow; the cooks with no other choice would fling the bits of batter left from a deep-fry with a plea, "hush, puppy!"

Bobby Sand's
⇒ Scones ⇐

1 1/2 cup whole wheat flour
2 tsp. baking powder
pinch salt
1/4 cup soy margarine
1/2 cup milk or soy milk
1 TBS. honey
1/3 cup raisins, chopped (optional)

This recipe is basically the same as that for baking powder biscuits. Mix the dry ingredients together and cut in the margarine. Make a well and pour in the milk, honey, and raisins. Mix rapidly to form a soft dough. Turn this onto a floured board and kneed it very slightly, until it feels right. The lightest touch produces the lightest scone. Roll the dough out about 3/4 inch thick. Cut with a biscuit cutter and place on a greased cookie sheet. Cut an "X" or a cross into the top of each scone with a sharp knife. If you have any milk left over you can brush the tops with it. Place on the lower rack of your oven at about 425^ (preheated), and bake for about 10 or 15 minutes. This recipe makes just enough for a cozy tea. If you want enough scones to have some left over for breakfast, double the recipe.

FLOUR TORTILLAS

When I make tortillas I flash back to an ancient lifetime, a brown wrinkled old lady squatting in front of a fire, rolling out tortillas on a rock. It seems every culture has its own version: crepes, strudel, pasta, shortbread, hoecakes, dumplings, chapati, biscuits, pancakes, knish, and pirogi. I love recipes that haven't changed in 5,000 years. Some are a lot easier than others, but most of them are pretty simple, made from basic peasant type food. Tortillas are my favorite, here's how to do it:

6 cups of flour (I use any combination of whole wheat, white, chapati flour)
1 tsp. salt
2 tsp. baking powder
1/4 cup plus 2 TBS. oil or melted margarine
warm water as needed

Mix the dry ingredients together in a bowl and make a well. Pour in the oil, then 1/2 cup warm water. Stir until well blended then add about 3/4 cup more water, till you think it's kneadable. Turn this onto a floured board and knead gently about 10 times. Cover with an apron or a dish towel and let rest about 5 minutes (at my house this usually turns into about 20 or 30 minutes as I am apt to sit and have a beer while getting ready for the big roll out). About 5 minutes before you're getting ready to start, get a dry cast iron skillet, put over low flame, and allow to get hot.

Break off a piece of dough, about the size between a walnut and a golf ball, roll it in flour and roll out on a floured board as thin as possible. Put this in the skillet and start on another. You may have to adjust the heat from medium to low while tor-

tillas are cooking. If you are getting them rolled out faster than they are getting done, turn up the heat a little or vice-versa. When the top of the tortilla has little bubbles and the bottom has brown flecks, turn it over with your fingers or a fork (don't poke or flatten tortilla). If you have two skillets or a griddle use them both; you will be able to get a real rhythm going. Stack the finished tortillas one by one on top of each other and cover with a cloth napkin. They'll stay nice and hot that way.

Vegetarians really go all out when eating stuffed tortillas. Here are some of the things I have put in mine:

beans (anykind), guacomole,mustard
chicken fried tofu, tempeh, tomatoes,
nutritional yeast, cucumbers, kelp
green onions, falafel, parmesan
hot peppers, (or any kind of cheese)

When Patsy, Dori, and I first got to Denver we were so poor we had to run down to the filling station on the corner to use their toilet paper. We had gotten a 50 lb. bag of flour from public assistance and we also had a benevolent neighbor who would occasionally bring big bags of cucumbers, tomatoes, and green onions from her garden. It took us about a minute to figure out how to put the vegetables to use. We had tortillas every night for weeks, and grew our own sprouts to put in as well (they take up lots of room). To say we ate like queens is putting it mildly. I have never been able to duplicate those burritos. Don't be limited by money when you fix dinner; it does not have to be a major factor.

SHADY SIDE NUT MUFFINS

1 1/4 cup whole wheat flour
1/2 cup any other flour (oat, rye, buckwheat, soy, etc.)
2 tsp. baking powder
1/2 tsp. salt
1/4 cup each of 3 kinds of nuts (you can use sesame seeds, walnuts, sliced or toasted almonds, pumpkin seeds, cashews, peanuts, etc.) chopped
1 egg or egg replacer
1 cup water or soymilk
3 TBS. oil
2 TBS. honey

If you want a sweeter muffin to use as a dessert or for tea, add 1/2 cup raisins or a chopped apple.

Mix the dry ingredients together and add the nuts, and raisins or apple.

Stir together the milk or water, egg, oil, and honey. Pour this into the dry ingredients all at once and stir until moist. Grease muffin tins and fill 3/4 full with batter. Bake at 350^ for 20 minutes. Serve hot with dinner or spread with jams for dessert.

Coffee Ridge Pineapple Nut Bread

2 1/4 cups flour (whole wheat or white)
3/4 cups honey
1 1/4 tsp. salt
2 tsp. baking powder
1 tsp. baking soda
1 cup wheat bran or wheat germ
1 cup chopped pecans or walnuts
1 1/2 cups pineapple, chopped very fine
2 TBS. pineapple juice
1 egg or egg replacer
3 TBS. oil or melted margarine
1/2 to 1 cup dark raisins
1 tsp. vanilla or 1 tsp. rum extract

Stir the dry ingredients together. In another bowl, mix the honey, oil, egg replacer, pineapple, juice and extract. Add this to the dry ingredients then stir in nuts and raisins. If it seems dry, add a little more pineapple juice.

Bake in a greased loaf pan at 350^ for 1 to 1 1/4 hours. A straw should come out clean when the bread is done.

After it cools (best to sit it on a wire rack), wrap it well in plastic wrap, then aluminum foil, and let it sit and mellow for 3 to 10 days.

This is a very rich loaf, more like cake than bread. It has a real holiday feel to it, and can be made in advance to age as a gift under someone's tree.

ROCK FORK DROP BISCUITS

1 1/2 cup whole wheat flour
1 1/4 cup white flour (unbleached) or soy flour
1 1/4 cup soy milk, milk, or 1/2 water-1/2 milk
3 tsp. baking powder
5 to 6 TBS. oil (safflower or sesame is good)
1 tsp. salt

This is a good biscuit to make when you are in a hurry; you don't have to roll them out.

Stir the dry ingredients together in a bowl. If you want to, stir in 1/4 to 1/2 cup of wheat germ now. Cut in oil. Add milk all at once and stir quickly till blended. Drop teaspoon fulls onto a greased cookie sheet. Bake at 400^ for about 12 to 15 minutes, till nice and brown on bottom.

Serve hot with any soup, beans, lots of gravy, breakfast, butter, honey, and jam with tea.

SHORT'NIN BREAD

Three little chil-uns, lyin' in bed,
two was sick and the other most dead,
Call for de' doctor, de' doc he said,
"You got feed dem chil-uns on some Short'nin
Bread."

Mammy's little baby love short'nin, short'nin,
Mammy's little baby loves short'nin bread.
Mammy's little baby love short'nin, short'nin,
Mammy's little baby loves short'nin bread.

When I made this at work one day, my friend Tina
came rushing into the kitchen. "These taste just
like what my neighbor in Boston, Mrs. Jamison,
used to make. When she gave me the recipe, she
told me it was handed down in her family since
the last great-great-grandmother that anyone
could remember; she called it Scotch Short Bread."

On close inspection, we discovered that Mrs.
Jamison used rice flour and I used whole wheat
but we both cut diamonds across the top. Tina
and I both got off on wondering where this recipe
might first have sprung up, but the fact that it's so
widely loved and simply made is reason enough
for you to try it.

**2 cups flour (rice, whole wheat, or any
combination)**
1/2 tsp. salt
**1/2 cup brown sugar or 1/4 cup plus 2 TBS.
honey, rice syrup, molasses, maple syrup, or
barley malt)**
**1 cup (2 sticks) butter or margarine (old time
recipes say don't substitute margarine for butter but I almost always do)**

Put the flour and salt in a bowl. Cut the margarine
in chunks and add it. Cut it in with a pastry
blender or 2 sharp knives. You want to do this
good, not till its like peas but more like cornmeal.
Stir in the honey with a fork until it becomes very
smooth—it shouldn't take too long. Put on a
cookie sheet or baking pan, ungreased, and press
down with fingers. Cut diamonds in the top,
baklava style. Prick with fork. Bake at 350^ for
about 20 minutes or until the shortbread is light
brown and starts to pull slightly away from the
edge of the pan.

P.S. Add 1 tsp. of vanilla if you like...

P.P.S. If you use brown sugar, add it with the flour
and cut in along with the butter.

LITTLE BURNS OFTEN LEAVE UGLY SCARS!

MAMMA'S FAMOUS CHEESEBREAD

At my house, this is as much a Christmas tradition as Granny's Red Velvet Cake. It is totally worth every bite. Crisped croutons made from this bread are not to be believed, and as a sandwich bread it can't be beat.

1/4 lb. swiss cheese
1/4 lb. sharp cheddar cheese
2 tsp. honey
1/4 tsp. salt
2 pkg. yeast
1 cup warm water
1 cup margarine
4 1/2 cups flour (mamma uses white, I mix white and whole wheat)
6 beaten eggs (egg replacer works very successfully in this)
1/2 cup grated Parmesan cheese

Let cheese sit out till room temperature; then cut into 1/4 inch cubes.

Mix flour and salt.

Dissolve the yeast in warm water and honey. Let sit 8 to 10 minutes.

Cream the margarine and eggs or replacer together, then add to yeast mixture. Gradually add flour while stirring. Stir in all the cheese toward the end of stirring. If you are doing this by hand (not in a mixer) you will have to knead about 5 minutes. You are aiming for a satiny-like sheene.

Turn into a greased bowl and let rise till doubled. Punch it down and let it rise again. It won't take as long this time. Turn into a greased bundt pan (for a fancy Christmas bread) or into 2 bread pans. Let rise again!

Bake at 350^ about 40 minutes. Let this cool about 30 minutes before you take it out of the pan. It's delicious hot or cold.

This is also a good bread to make when it's cold out and you want to be in a nice warm kitchen all day. It can turn a plain cabbage or noodle soup into a memorable occasion.

BUNS!! BUNS!!

If you are already a bread maker then you can skip this part. But if you are one of the few remaining people who still think bread making is too hard, too time consuming, boring, old-fashioned, sissyfied, meesy, tedious, hippie-fied, or old maidish—STOP!!!...this is a citizen's arrest. Go in the kitchen right now, get out a bowl, put on an apron and you're off, second star to the left and straight on till morning.

This will be a step by step recipe for how to make bread. It's like learning to swim: once you've done it, you never forget how and it's always the same...it just gets easier and more fun.

To make these buns you'll need:
1 cup warm water
1 PKG. yeast
1 tsp. honey
1 tsp. salt
1/2 cup oil
3 cups whole wheat flour any combination of white and whole wheat if you'd like)
2 TBS. sesame seeds

Okay, first you do the yeast part. Some recipes just say dissolve yeast in warm water and stir in the flour. This really isn't fair to you or the yeast. If you do that, the yeast can't perform and you end up with rock hard buns. (Just when you don't want rock hard buns, you get them!) If you do this right, not only will your yeast perform, you'll get an Acadamy Award winning role right there in your kitchen. You need 1 cup of warm water (read closely, this can be a tricky part), not scalding hot but not tepid. Run the water over the inside of your wrist. It should feel nice and warm;

a little on the hot side. So, go ahead and dissolve the yeast in the water. The yeast will come to life, and like all living things, it'll need food. Stir in a tsp. or so of honey or mayple syrup. Now just let it happen. I love to watch this, it's like life on fast forward. It takes about 10 minutes to fully develop and still not loose it's oomph. Be careful not to let the yeast go more than about 10 minutes though, because it will max itself out of existence.

Stir in about 1/2 the flour, yeast, and oil. Stir this around just to get it going, then add the rest of the flour and stir 200 strokes. (This can be measured by the time it takes your arm to just about fall off). Also, if you want to add anything extra to this bread, do it now (herbs, chopped onion, poppy seeds, sesame seeds, raisins, cheese, etc.).

Lightly flour a board and turn the dough out onto it. Do this on a counter or table space that's good for your size and gives you a little elbow room. You are ready to knead! Push the heal of your hand down on top half of the dough, fold it over and give the whole a 1/4 to 1/2 turn. Keep pushing, folding, and turning for about 5 minutes (most breads take a little longer than this). It should be shiny, smooth, and elastic when it's done (don't be afraid to sprinkle on a little more flour if you need to).

Grease a big bowl with margarine or oil and turn the dough into it. Cover it with an apron or a dish towel...you get the picture. Put this in a warm place and let it rise. This should take about an hour; it'll double in size. Uncover it, make a fist and give it the old Marvelous Marvin knock-out punch.

Now, I'm going to tell you how to make buns. If you want to, you can put this dough in muffin tins; you can shape them into skinny, individual loaves; or you can make 8 little balls and place them close together and sprinkle with poppy seeds to make real Italian dinner rolls. But...I know a way of making buns that works better than any assembly line factory machine ever, and the way they pop out of your hands is so cute. Oil your hands, grab a handful of dough and roll in your hands. Try to get all the dough in 1 hand and give it a hard squeeze; the object is to keep your fingers tight and the dough will pop out through the top of your hand by your thumb and index finger. You may need a couple of practice pops but it won't take more than that before you are popping out little buns faster than Sunbeam Bakery. Pop them onto a greased cookie sheet and sprinkle the tops with sesame seeds if you want. Let these sit about 5 or 10 minutes before putting them in a preheated 350^ oven. If you are in a hurry, you don't have to wait. Bake these for about 10 minutes or until the bottoms are brown and the tops are turning golden.

I love these buns. If you can't find any good ones at your grocery store, these are worth making and no burger or carrot dog is really complete without one.

Easy Overnight Cinnamon Rolls

This is a good recipe for someone who is really serious about having cinnamon rolls for breakfast. Most of the hard part is done the day or night before, and you can finish them while you are wandering around making coffee the next morning. I like to use this recipe, otherwise my cinnamon rolls aren't ready before dessert at suppertime.

Okay, use the recipe from Mom's refrigerator rolls. Go ahead and put in the fridge, just like it says. The next morning remove from fridge. First thing, let it sit about 20 minutes, so it will be workable. Roll it out into a big rectangle about 1/4 to 1/2 inch thick.

Spread with:
soft margarine or butter (add to suit yourself)
sprinkle with brown sugar or drizzle with honey (lots)
chopped nuts
sprinkle with about 1 tsp. cinnamon

Roll up like a jelly roll, take a sharp knife and slice off 1 inch sections. Place in a greased casserole, fairly close together, not touching. Brush with a little more margarine or honey if you want. Cover and let rise about 1/2 to 1 hour until doubled. Bake in a 375^ oven for 15 to 20 minutes, until golden and done.

If the smell of coffee and cinnamon rolls doesn't get everyone out of bed, nothing will.

Mom's Dining Room Refrigerator Rolls

The best thing about these rolls is that they're easy and so good I've seen people eat eight or nine at one sitting. I always make these when I don't have time to fool around in the kitchen before a party. Since the batter rises in the refrigerator you can mix them up the day before and have the biggest part done.

1/2 cup margarine
1 cup warm water (for yeast)
1/4 cup honey
3 to 4 cups flour
1 tsp. salt
1 pkg. or 1 TBS. yeast
1/2 cup boiling water
1/2 stick melted margarine
1 egg or egg replacer or butter

You can use any combination of white or whole wheat flour in these rolls. 100% whole wheat works fine.

Pour boiling water over the margarine, honey, and salt. Blend and let this cool. Add the egg or replacer. Dissolve the yeast in warm water and let it do its thing. Add the activated yeast to the rest of the mixture. Mix in the flour with about 200 strokes. Put in a well greased bowl and place in the refrigerator with a damp cloth on top.

Once when I was making these, our refrigerator blew up (not due to the rolls), so I just put them on the back porch in a big snowstorm and it worked just fine. You don't have to leave it overnight—4 hours at least, and 2 days at the most.

About 3 hours before needed, take the dough out of the refrigerator (or out of the cold) and let it sit for about 20 minutes (if you try to work with it right away, it'll be hard too handle). Roll the dough to about 1/4 inch thick. Melt 1/2 stick of butter. Cut out circles in the dough with a biscuit cutter or a wide mouth jar or glass (at least 2 inches across). Dip one flat side of each piece into the melted butter and fold over, butter side in. Place these close together on a cookie sheet and brush the tops lightly with the remaining butter. Let them sit about 1and1/2 hours. Bake at 425^ for 12 to 15 minutes, or until the bottoms are browned.

If, perchance, you have any of these left over, they're great toasted for breakfast with jam and tea.

IZZIE COHEN'S BAGELS

1 1/2 cup potato water
1 TBS. honey
1 pkg. yeast
6 cups flour (any mixture of whole wheat and unbleached white is fine)
1/4 cup oil
1 tsp. salt
1 egg or egg replacer
1 big pot of boiling water
toppings for bagels: poppy seeds, sesame seeds, finely chopped onion and/or garlic

Dissolve yeast and honey in potato water. Let sit for about 8 minutes. Stir in half of the flour until it is well mixed. Add the rest of the flour and the rest of the ingredients and give it about 200 strokes. Turn onto a board and kneed about 8 to 10 minutes. This is a very stiff dough so don't worry about it—add only enough flour to the board to keep it from sticking.

Put in a greased bowl, cover it, and let sit for one hour.

Punch down. Break off a piece of dough, roll out like a fat pencil. Press ends together and let rise about 30 minutes. Put risen side down in boiling water (you can add a touch of honey to the water if you want). Let boil 30 seconds to 1 minute on each side, covered. Keep the water rapidly boiling.

Shake a little corn meal over a cookie sheet (or grease it). Place bagels on the cookie sheet and sprinkle with seeds, onions, etc. Bake at 350^ for 25 to 30 minutes or till nice and brown.

English✶*Muffins*

Licorice flopped down on a big chair in the corner and looked at Patsy. She was spreading a cloth on the kitchen table. Licorice had been brooding ever since she'd gotten to the ranch and was driving Patsy crazy. "I've never seen you as love sick as this, Licorice honey, is it a man or a woman? "

Licorice took a long drag on her joint and blew it out in a big puff before she answered, "It's like my life is out of control–*Girl goes over Niagara Falls in a barrel*. Not that I want to be in control, just the standing eight count before the knock out punch, that's all." Patsy handed her an ashtray and Licorice carefully placed the roach on the edge, "... and besides, whose to say my songs are about violence?"
"Why, who said that? " cried Patsy. "I knew it, I just knew it, Licorice. It's that big city and that damn guitar that led you straight to the pits. You better mark my words- when push comes to shove, those new friends of yours are gonna shove. They're gonna shove you right in the pits."
Licorice leaned back in her chair, a Kool in the side of her mouth and watched Patsy through half closed eyes. She was bent over the stove, trying to get the heat right on a burner - when it finally suited her, she scooted a skillet over it. Patsy turned and reached in the cabinet, and began setting plates and silverware on the table. There was a serving spoon that had acorns and oak leaves all over it; a little spoon, it's handle looked like the Empire State Building. Tea cups made their way off of hooks and onto the table along with Licorice's all time favorite tea pot. It was shaped like an elephant and the lid was a little boy holding a parasol. Next came the napkins; Patsy always used real napkins. One had lace around the edge and it reminded Licorice of something you would carry in a wedding for the "something old

and borrowed" part. Out came a little pot with roses and gold trim on the sides, full of raspberry jam. Saucers with butter appeared; a jar of sourwood honey.
"That guitar meant trouble from the start," Patsy was talking to herself, "I mean big trouble."
She usually had at least 5 or 6 salt shakers on the table at any one time. Of course, only one or two ever had any salt in them, they just kept Patsy company. There was a little frog, a cowboy boot (written on one side was " I get a kick out of Texas,") an Indian brave in a canoe, and a real Classic of Elvis Presley leaning over belting it out (Patsy always put this one by Licorice's plate.)

There was something about the way Patsy was setting the table and tending the stove that Licorice couldn't quite put her finger on the same way she had always been able to put her fingers so deliberately on a certain chord. The more she watched Patsy, the better she felt though.
The sun was coming in the window over the kitchen sink, but it was nothing compared to the light that was there when she closed her eyes.
"What I have to do," she thought to herself, "is to stop beating the thing inside of me that wants to feel love..."

1 cup warm potato water
1/2 cup hot milk or soy milk
3 TBS oil or margarine
3 1/2 cups flour (half whole wheat/ half white is fine)
1 pkg. yeast
1 TBS honey
1 tsp. salt

Dissolve the yeast in the potato water with honey. Let it sit about 10 minutes. Stir in the milk and half the flour. You don't knead this, but instead give it a good stir. Use a wire whip if you want because this is more like a batter. Let this sit for 1 1/2 to 2 hours until it falls back on itself. Stir in the rest of the flour, and the oil and salt. For the second rising, let the muffins rise in their tins on a griddle. You can find traditional tins at gourmet stores, or antique shops. You can also use empty fish tins that have been cleaned well. Sprinkle a little corn meal on a barely greased cold griddle. Let the muffins rise till twice their size. If you use real muffin tins, just fill them up 1/2 way. If you use fish tins, just fill them 1/4 of the way. If these are filled too full, the muffins will stay doughy in the middle. When doubled, slide the griddle onto a low flame, and check the bottom of the muffins by barely lifting them up with a spatula. You only want to turn these over once. Don't grease the skillet again unless you have too. The muffins should take about 15 minutes to cook. Let cool and remove from the tins. Also, when you are moving the muffins to the griddle, or tuning them over, be careful not to drop or jostle them as the air will poof out of them and they won't be as good. These cook sort of like pancakes in that little holes will appear on the top and tell you that it is time to turn them over, These are fun, but if you've never made bread before, don't start with this recipe.

PROPERLY MADE TEA

NO 1 Start with freshly drawn water. You don't have to go to the well, but don't use the same water that's been sitting on the stove all day.

NO 2 Rinse out your teapot with very hot water (to warm it up as well as clean it).

NO 3 Go ahead and now put the tea leaves in the pot. The heat from the pot will make the leaves begin to release their aroma and start doing their thing.

NO 4 When the water comes to a rolling boil, it's ready (not when it starts to bubble a little bit, and not when it's been boiling for 15 minutes). The longer water boils, the more oxygen it looses, and this makes it taste flat. Pour the water over the tea leaves and cover the pot. Let steep for 3 to 5 minutes depending on how strong you like it. Some herb teas can brew up to 15 minutes without turning bitter. Black teas don't take nearly as long.

It's a good thing to know how to make tea the right way. You never know when Chrissie Hynde is going to drop by for tea, and she doesn't like to drink tea unless it's done right.

A LITTLE SOMETHING FOR A TRUCK DRIVING MAN

Turnovers *Empanadas

Packing A Lunch

Captain Freedom's Special *(A Hero Sandwich)*

Gooey's Special

BAG LUNCHES FOR BAG LADIES

Samauri Sushi

Steven's Sushi

Stuffed Peppers A La Appalachian

Castroville's Contribution

Empanadas Filled Turnovers

1 cup Texturized Vegetable Protein
1 cup boiling water
2 TBS. tamari
salt and pepper
1 onion, chopped fine
2 cloves garlic
1/2 cup parsley
1 hard boiled egg, chopped (optional)
1 cup peas
2 TBS. ketchup
1/2 tsp. cumin

PASTRY:
1 1/2 cup pastry flour
1 TBS. baking powder
1/2 tsp. salt
1/3 cup margarine
1/3 cup warm water
1 tsp. lemon juice

Make the pastry first and let it sit in the fridge while you make the filling. Mix the dry ingredients together and stir into the flour till it makes a ball. Wrap in waxed paper and put in fridge.

Now, put the TVP in a medium bowl. Bring 1 cup of water to a boil and stir in ketchup, tamari, salt, pepper, and cumin. Pour over TVP, cover, and let stand about 15 minutes. Brown the onion and a little oil in a skillet. Add TVP mixture, stirring often so it won't stick. The last few minutes add the peas and parsley. Then remove from heat and stir in chopped egg if you are using it.

Now you're ready to roll. On a well floured board, roll out pastry and cut out in circles. They should be about 5 inches across. You can use a saucer to help you get it right. Put a heaping spoonful (it doesn't take much) of filling and put it just barely under the halfway mark. Then fold over and pinch edges together with your fingers or with the tips of a fork. Barely brush the tops with melted margarine. Unless you're taking them on a trip, cut a little crows foot design in the top. Place on a cookie sheet and bake in a 400^ preheated oven for about 15 minutes of until brown.

This is a perfect special something for road trips or to wrap in a big bandana the next time you run away from home.

⋙ PACKING A LUNCH ⋘

I don't think this chapter would be complete without a tribute to grandmother's everywhere and especially my grandmothers, who both happen to be masters of the packed lunch. Whether you were just taking a bagged lunch to school, or something to eat half way to Myrtle Beach on the family vacation (We always ate at Sweat Bee Haven) these lunches rate as the best ever. God, what memories. I can see that box now, all tied up and so heavy. Could all this be food?

There was fried chicken, I loved it then, cheese sandwiches, the kind with grated onion and mayo; deviled eggs screwed back together and wrapped in wax paper with twisted ends. Carrot curls made with a vegetable peeler packed in baggies with ice cubes. Grandma Sarah always used those little papers you use to line muffin tins to hold wonderful little surprises: chocolate almonds, raisins, toasted salted nuts. In those lunches, nothing was ever soggy. She also added the unexpected: note paper, pencils, emery boards, paper clips, and maps. Yes, all this in a lunch. There were always lots of napkins, silverware and handiwipes.

The brownies were in a small box all wrapped up inside the big one. Granny made a big batch of praline cookies and these were kept in a separate cookie tin and were therefore lots easier to snitch. If all this is making you hungry, why don't you pack a big lunch and zoom off on a big adventure right now.

CAPTAIN FREEDOM'S SPECIAL

(A Hero Sandwich)

2 avocados, peeled and sliced thin
1 tomato sliced (if you like tomato)
sesame salt as needed (see recipe below)
mayonnaise
dijon mustard
2 TBS. crumbled blue cheese (optional)
pita or whole wheat sliced bread (really any bread works well, but you get more to eat if you use pita)

I listed all the ingredients that I like on this sandwich, but it's just as good with only avocado, mayo, and sesame salt. This is also a great sandwich to grill.

Here's how to make sesame salt: Toast about 1 cup sesame seed over a low flame in a cast iron skillet; you'll be able to smell them. If they start popping, you have the flame turned up too high; turn it down a little. I like to let mine get real dark, not burnt, just well roasted. When the sesame seeds get about 1/2 done, add about 2 tsp. salt. There are many theories about how much salt to use; some say 1 part salt to 16 parts seeds, I don't know what this works out to, but I know I don't like mine too salty. After you make this once, you'll know how you like it. Let the salt and seeds finish cooking together. You can grind this in a blender till it looks like course salt or do it by hand in a serabachi (that's one of those little bowls with the grooves in the bottom). Sesame salt will keep in an air tight container. It's one of my favorite condiments. Try it on sandwiches, popcorn, soup, toast, muffins, bagels, baked potatoes, baked squash, noodles, rice, salad, and sushi. It tastes like bacon bits.

135

GOOEY'S SPECIAL

Hitchhikers sometimes have strange hours and Gooey, being the most famous hitchhiker of all time, is apt to have the strangest ones of all. You may want to have this sandwich ready for her when she gets home from a long, wet, five day hitch. Or, ready in a paper sack for her to grab on her way out the door in the middle of the night.

2 to 4 slices leftover chicken fried tofu
(this has to be leftover in the fridge
for at least one night)
bread
very thinly sliced raw onion
mayonnaise
tomatoes (if you're going to be eating
this on the road, omit the tomatoes)

Toast the bread if you want and spread with mayonnaise. Add the sliced onion, tomato, and tofu. This sandwich is so good, and I really encourage you to try this recipe. The only hard part is this: everyone, including me, likes chicken fried tofu so much, there's never any left over. Maybe you should make twice the amount.

"Hey girl, get with it in there, that ol' highway's a callin'." Licorice had a big mirror propped up against a tree in the backyard and was respiking her hair. There were snips and locks flying all around her head, covering her shoulders and the better part of her boots.

Patsy didn't know why she always worked so hard on Licorice's lunches. Deep down inside she felt like Licorice probably left the whole thing in the back seat of the first ride she got. Deeper down, she thought about Licorice going to bed hungry and cold. Oh. Darn these good-byes anyway. A big tear rolled down her cheek and plopped into the brownie mix and Patsy stirred harder than ever.

"Hold your horses, I'm still packing."

Patsy had just found the right box to pack everything in and the food was just about ready. A big shoe box of chocolate chip-oatmeal cookies went on the bottom along with a pencil and a couple of self addressed stamped postcards. Once one of these had actually come back, and even though there was nothing written on it ,of course Patsy knew who it was from. Next, beside the cookies went a container of cold fried chicken tofu, 1/2 a loaf of home made salt risen bread, and a small jar of Hellman's. A big bag of fruit went right on top of the cookies, and then four steamed artichokes went in along side that. She completely filled the box with: pickled eggs wrapped in wax paper with the ends twisted, cupcake papers filled with roasted nuts, almonds and cashews, the leftover stuffed peppers from last night's dinner, 2 crunchy nut muffins and 2 tofu biscuits. Patsy always put in two of everything because she knew Licorice liked to offer the people who picked her up some of whatever she had. The brownies were just cool enough to cut, wrap and put on the top. She covered the whole thing with a table cloth, a napkin, and slipped in a salt shaker and silverware on the side.

"Why is it," Patsy looked up, "We are always saying good-bye and why does it have to be that way?"

"You know better than to ask that question. You know why. We got to feel our lives, to really feel them. Not just tip-toe around on egg shells like we're scared to make a noise. It's like we don't have choice. Just like there is something in you that's gotta cook, there is something in me that has gotta sing. I guess you could say it's almost as if we were driven."

"Driven???", Patsy said nervously. She didn't drive and was instantly suspicious of any suggestion that she might have to. Patsy stopped crying and had started to blow her nose which was a good sign.

Licorice took advantage of this pause and said, "Yeah and uh speaking of driving, I better make tracks."

"Oh, you and your old tracks anyway!!" They walked to the front porch hand in hand, gave each other a hug and kiss that could only be described as fierce. Patsy heard something boiling over in the kitchen and she ran there to see about it. When she got the mess cleaned up and herself back to the porch, Licorice and her lunch were gone.

Samauri Sushi

2 or 3 cups cooked brown rice
1 medium zucchini
1/4 cabbage, sliced very fine
1/2 onion, chopped
1 or 2 carrots, grated
3 or 4 umeboshi plums
1 TBS. grated ginger
3 cloves garlic, minced
2 tsp. thyme
tamari
salt and pepper
4 or 5 sheets of nori

Heat oil in skillet and add chopped onion and garlic. Then add cabbage, zucchini, and carrots and let cook a few minutes, stirring with a wooden spoon. add the ginger, thyme, salt, pepper, and tamari. Cover and simmer about 5 minutes or until soft. While the vegetables are cooking, toast the nori over a small flame on your stove (electric burners work too!). This will turn a lighter green color and you'll smell it. It takes just a second for each one. If you've never had this before, don't be shy; it's really good.

Lightly mix the rice and vegetables together in a bowl. Place a piece of toasted nori lengthwise in front of you. Place a small amount of rice and vegetables on one end of the nori and spread it to both sides. Take a small amount of umeboshi paste, or pull the meat off the plum and spread a thin line down the length of the rice mixture. Roll up the sushi and dab water on one end to make it stick. You can crispen these up again if you want to. These are nice served in bite sized pieces, or if you are taking them on a trip, wrap them separately in a plastic bag. They will keep well on the road as the pickled plum will preserve it.

STEVEN'S SUSHI

There are as many ways to make sushi as there are to make sandwiches. This one is easy and it has always been Steven's favorite.

2 cups cooked rice
1 or 2 TBS. rise vinegar
tahini
umeboshi paste
nori, 3 or 4 sheets

Pour vinegar over rice and toss. Toast nori over flame or burner. Place several spoonfuls of rice over the bottom part of the nori. Spread on some tahini the way you'd spread mustard on a hot dog. Do the same with umeboshi paste, but don't use quite as much. Roll up. Make as many as you have ingredients for.

Remember, this is good for a quick lunch. Sushi makes a great traveling food too. Wrap them separately in saran, and put your hammer down.

Stuffed Peppers ≈a la≈ Appalachian

6 large green peppers
2 cups leftover rice (also millet, noodles, any cooked grain will do)
1 onion, chopped
2 carrots, grated
1 block tofu
1/2 cup nutritional yeast
1/2 tsp. dry mustard
1/4 cup sesame seeds
2 TBS. oil
tamari and pepper

Stuffed peppers are perfect for bag lunches because you can make them the day before, they freeze well, they taste better the next day anyway, and you eat the container they come in.

Believe me, if the peppers are not cooked, people will eat the stuffing and throw the peppers away. Barely slice the top off each pepper and reserve. Scoop out the pulp and seeds and throw away. Put the peppers cut side down in a pan with just a little water. Steam until they turn bright green, then remove from heat and leave covered until you need them. This just takes a few minutes.

Heat the sesame seeds in oil until they start to pop, then add onions, carrots, garlic, and tamari. Cook till tender but not done.

Chop tofu. Add this to the simmering vegetables. Then add everything to the leftover rice and mix up real good. Stuff into the steamed peppers. Put these upright in a casserole dish. Some people like a slice of cheese on top, but I like a dot of butter with breadcrumbs.

If you want, put a pan of water in the bottom of the oven so these can steam. Bake about 30 minutes at 350^.

CASTROVILLE'S CONTRIBUTION

Ah, yes Castroville—the artichoke capital of the world. Artichokes are the perfect food for bag ladies of any nation. Oddly elegant, they can be plucked, scraped, and savored on any leisurely stroll from Colfax Avenue to Hollywood Boulevard, benches from Central Park West to Squirrel Hill, bus stops, curbs, (bag ladies are very discriminating you'll find) There's a bonus...since you'll throw the leaves away, and eat the heart and stem, you'll have an extra bag to add to your collection when you rearrange them after lunch.

3 or 4 artichokes, or as many as you can eat small 69 cent jar of mayonnaise from corner store— hot lemon garlic butter is good too and so is blue cheese dressing but if you are on the move, the mayo could be easiest (if you've never had plain mayo on artichokes, you haven't lived)

Cut the tips of the artichokes (unless you think you need them for protection.) Steam them for 45 minutes. See if you can pull out a leaf, if you can, scrape the pulp and see how tender it is. These are good hot or cold. Steam them in the morning while you finish packing, and have them for lunch 400 miles later.

SWEETS

Swannanoa Shortcake

Great Aunt Alzenia's Brownies

Mama's Dark Secret

Patsy's Own Peanut Butter Blossoms

Chocolate Chip Cookies

Cupid's Thumbprint

Susan's Apple Crisp

Cranberry Frappé And About Sherbert

Prissy's Easy Peach Cobbler

Seven Layer Cookies

Agar-Agar

Old Fashioned Gingerbread

War Cake

Mini*Ha*Ha Cake And Frosting

Tootie's Praline Cookies

Annie's Chocolate Almond Cookies

"AH, YOU FLAVOR EVERYTHING;
YOU ARE THE VANILLA
OF SOCIETY."
SYDNEY SMITH 1771-1845

"HEAVEN SENDS US GOOD FOOD,
BUT THE DEVIL SENDS GOOD
COOKS."
DAVID GARRICK 1716-1779

"THE ONLY WAY TO GET RID OF
TEMPTATION IS TO YIELD TO IT."
OSCAR WILDE 1856-1900

SWANNANOA SHORTCAKE

This shortcake whips up very fast and is good to have with any fruit in season. I like to use peaches or blueberries or black berries not just strawberries.

2 cups flour
3 tsp. baking powder
1 tsp. salt
1/3 cup margarine
1 cup milk or soymilk
2 TBS. honey

Mix the dry ingredients together, then cut in the margarine until it becomes the consistency of cornmeal. Stir in the milk all at once, quickly, till just blended. Press into a greased pan. Dot with margarine and bake at 400^ for 12 to 15 minutes. Cut into nice-sized squares and serve with your favorite fruit. Strawberries, pineapple, blackberries, raspberries, or peaches are all good.

P.S. If you miss whipped cream and want something to pour over your shortcake, here is a good fruit glaze:

1/2 to 1 cup fruit
1/4 cup cold water
1 TBS. honey
1 tsp. kudzu

Smash fruit with a potato masher, just till they start to bleed a little. Put in a saucepan with honey. Dissolve the kudzu in cold water and add to the fruit. Stir over medium heat till thickened. Let cool and serve over any shortcake.

Great Aunt Alzenia's Brownies

3/4 cup flour
1/4 tsp. salt
1/4 tsp. baking powder
3/4 cup honey
1/2 cup margarine
2 eggs or replacer
3 squares unsweetened chocolate or
3 TBS. cocoa or
3 TBS. carob powder
1 tsp. vanilla
1 cup walnuts or pecans, chopped

Melt the margarine in a sauce pan and then add honey and cocoa or whatever your using. Remove from heat and let cool a few minutes. Quickly stir in eggs, vanilla, and salt. Then fold in flour and nuts. Don't stir this too much, but make sure it's smooth. Pour in a greased square pan and put in a preheated 350^ oven. These bake about 30 minutes. This is one recipe where the toothpick test doesn't really work. I like brownies chewy, but anyway, after about 25 minutes, take them out of the oven and check them. Press your finger lightly to the middle. You'll know if it's too gooey and not done. They should be about done, but if you have to leave them in another 5 minutes, go ahead. Be sure not to overbake though, as they will become dried out. When you take them out, let them sit about 30 minutes before you cut them.

This is a great recipe for a small batch of brownies. If you want a lot or even just a big pan, you should double or triple this recipe.

Mamma's Dark Secret

2 cups flour (unbleached white works best)
1 1/2 cup brown sugar
2 sticks butter or margarine
4 TBS. cocoa (or carob)
1 cup coffee
2 eggs or egg replacer
1/2 cup buttermilk
1 tsp. vanilla
1 tsp. baking soda

Stir the flour and salt together in a bowl. Put the butter, cocoa, and coffee in a sauce pan and bring just to a boil. Stir in the honey. When the honey is dissolved, pour all this over the dry ingredients and mix well. Beat in the eggs, the buttermilk, and vanilla. Add the soda last. Pour into a greased and floured pan. Use a rectangular pan, about 10 by 15 inches as this is a sheet cake. Sometimes I use 2 pie plates. Bake for 30 minutes at 350^ or till a straw comes out clean when stuck in the middle.

FROSTING:
4 TBS. cocoaa
1 to 1 1/2 cup powdered milk
6 TBS. milk
1 tsp. vanilla
1 stick butter
1 1/2 cup chopped toasted pecans
1/2 cup honey or almonds, or both

While the cake is baking, make the icing. Bring the butter, cocoa, and milk just to boiling. Remove from heat and add the vanilla and honey. Stir in the powdered milk with a whip; add it slowly to make sure it doesn't lump. Stir in the toasted nuts. Pour this over the cake while the cake is still hot. Mamma tells me this is the secret.

143

Patsy's Own Peanut Butter Blossoms

1 3/4 cup flour
1/2 tsp. salt
1 tsp. baking soda
1/2 cup margarine
3/4 cup honey
1/2 cup peanut butter
1 egg or egg replacer
2 TBS. soymilk or water
1 tsp. vanilla
chocolate or carob kisses

Mix the flour, salt, and baking soda in a bowl. Cream margarine, honey, and peanut butter in another bowl and when smooth, add egg replacer, vanilla, soymilk, and stir again till smooth. Blend in the dry ingredients. Roll in the palms of your hands until you have round balls like walnuts. Place on ungreased cookie sheet and bake about 8 minutes. Then remove from the oven and press kiss into middle of ball until the edges crack a little and bake about 4 minutes more. These may seem like the kind of cookie you can't make unless you are a grandmother, but they're Patsy's favorites and believe me, she's no grandmother.

CHOCOLATE CHIP ~COOKIES~

2 1/4 cup whole wheat flour
 (unbleached works okay too)
1 tsp. baking soda
1 tsp. salt
1 cup soft margarine
3/4 cup honey
1/2 cup molasses, maple syrup, barley malt, brown sugar (or more honey)
1 tsp. vanilla
2 eggs or egg replacer
one small package of chocolate chips (semi-sweet are best)_
or carob chips
1 cup walnuts or pecans, chopped (any nut will do)

I LOVE chocolate chip cookies. I could even eat them for breakfast and have done so n many occasions. This is a fool-proof recipe. If you don't want them too sweet, just leave out the molasses. This cookie turns out like a really sweet bread; we jokingly call it the muffin cookie. This is also a good recipe to experiment with.

In a large bowl, cream the margarine and sweetener. Make sure this is smooth and not lumpy. Whip in vanilla and egg replacer until smooth. In another smaller bowl, mix together the flour, soda, and salt and then add this to the creamed mixture. Stir in the flour, soda, and salt and then add this to the creamed mixture. Stir in the nuts and chocolate chips. Drop on an ungreased cookie sheet and bake in a preheated 350^ oven till brown on the bottom—about 10 minutes.

At the warehouse, it never mattered what kind of cookie I made. someone would wander into the kitchen and say, "Hey, why don't these have any chocolate chips in them?"

At first, I gave what I considered to be a normal response, like, "Well, these are carrot raisin cookies," or "these are apple apricot cookies." Later, I learned that to most people, a cookie just isn't a cookie without chocolate chips. When in Rome...soon I was dumping bags of chocolate chips into everything, no matter what the recipe. Here are some of the variations that have worked for me.

№1

Add 1 1/2 cup oatmeal and 1 1/2 cup raisins to the original recipe.

№2

Cream 1/2 to 1 cup peanut butter with margarine and honey in original recipe. Or substitute peanuts for walnuts, or just use crunchy peanut butter and forget about the nuts altogether.

№3

Add 1 cup coconut to the original recipe.

№4

Once I was in a hurry and didn't have time to cream the honey and margarine by hand, so I melted it on the stove real fast. Anyway, when I mixed it all up together it was still warm and it started to meltyucky, but the cookies were delicious—a dark, rich, brown with tiny bits of chips left inside. I got more comments on these cookies; everyone loved them.

№5

If I have a little coffee left over in my cup, I go ahead and pour it in when I'm creaming the honey and margarine.

№6

Substitute 2 TBS. Kaluha, Jack Daniels, Ammeretto, or whatever liquor you like for the vanilla.

№7

1 to 1 1/2 cup any dry cereal you have on hand (rice crispies, corn flakes, wheaties, bran flakes) added to the dry ingredients will make a very crunchy cookie.

№8

If you are in a big hurry, just spread all the batter in the bottom of a pie plate or casserole dish and bake like a bar cookie.

CUPID'S THUMBPRINTS

1/2 cup margarine
2 TBS. brown sugar
3 TBS. honey or maple syrup
1 egg or egg replacer
1/2 tsp. vanilla
1 cup flour
1/4 tsp. salt
1/2 tsp. baking soda
red raspberry or strawberry jam
1/4 to 1/2 cup sesame seeds

Mix the margarine, sweeteners, egg, and vanilla till smooth. In another bowl, mix the dry ingredients, but not the sesame seeds. Then add to the wet ingredients. Be careful not to over stir. Roll a spoonful into a ball and roll in sesame seeds. Place 1" apart on ungreased cookie sheet and press thumb into the center of each. Bake at 350^ for 10 to 12 minutes or until brown on bottom. Fill with red raspberry or strawberry jam. These cookies are exquisite and look beautiful on a plate. They are very fancy little cookies.

P.S. If you don't use brown sugar, use about 1/3 cup of honey.

SUSAN'S APPLE CRISP

Once, in leaner times, Susan and Patsy both had jobs as waitresses at a place called Allen's Harem Lounge. It was the kind of place that some guy left a $100 tip on your day off. It specialized in hot soups and Allen's Famous Cornbread. Since Allen spent most of his time at his bookie's, most of the responsibility of running the place was left to Marge. She was the kind of lady who ran 1 1/2 hours late. Sometimes things could get a little out of hand at the Harem Lounge.

Marge would usually get to work about 5 minutes before the first customer. She would race around like a maniac, her apron on, ladle in one hand, a Kool extra long in the other, shouting orders like, "Quick, chop 12 onions" or "I need 2 bunches of parsley minced." Of course, as soon as you tried to chop the onions Marge would run frantically by again and say, "What are you doing that for? Hurry up and make the apple crisp!"

Marge always swore that Susan made the best apple crisp of anyone who ever worked there. So here it is from the Harem Lounge via Susan— Apple Crisp. This recipe will make a lot—enough for your family and a neighbor's too, or a big pot luck, or a picnic. If you don't need this much, just cut it in half.

6 lbs. apples cut up peeled (if you want), Susan says tart work the best but she usually used whatever Marge got on sale at the nearest grocery store
2 tsp. cinnamon
1 cup brown sugar (or 3/4 cup honey)

Mix the apples with the cinnamon and brown sugar and place in a baking dish. Be sure to use a glass dish and not a metal one because the metal will discolor the apples.

You have 3 choices for the topping:

 1

2 cups whole wheat flour
2 cups butter or margarine
pinch salt

 2

1 cup whole wheat flour
1 cup oats
2 cups butter or margarine

 3

1 cup whole wheat flour
1/2 cup oats
1/2 cup wheat germ
2 cups butter or margarine

Mix together with your hands until it's crumbly. To this, add 2 cups brown sugar or 1 1/2 cups honey (keep mixing). Pack this down on the apples and bake—the cooking time is questionable. Susan said she would make the crisp, put it in the oven, and start waiting on tables. Mid-way through the first lunch rush she would see Marge drop whatever she was doing, run wildly to the kitchen, nose to the air sniffing like a bloodhound. "Ahhhh, get the apple crisp—it's going to burn!" Usually it never burned, it was done just about the time the first customer was ready for dessert. Susan says estimate it at about 45 to 50 minutes at 350^.

TOOTIE'S PRALINE COOKIES

1/2 cup butter or margarine
1 2/3 cups unbleached white flour
1 1/2 tsp. baking powder
1/2 tsp. salt
3/4 cups white sugar
3/4 cups brown sugar, packed (if you're totally opposed to brown sugar, use molasses; it'll still work but the cookies won't taste like Tootie's)
1 egg or egg replacer
1 tsp. vanilla
1 cup pecans, chopped (you can leave these whole and press   into the top of the cookies before baking if you want)

Sift flour with baking powder and salt.

Cream margarine. Add brown sugar gradually, then egg or replacer, vanilla. Stir in the dry ingredients last (including the chopped pecans).

Drop by spoonfuls onto a greased cookie sheet and bake at 350^ for 10 to 12 minutes.

This cookie is the greatest and one of the few that you don't miss the chocolate chips.

CRANBERRY FRAPPÉ
AND
HOW TO MAKE SHERBERT

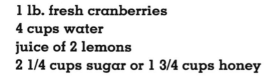

1 lb. fresh cranberries
4 cups water
juice of 2 lemons
2 1/4 cups sugar or 1 3/4 cups honey

Cook the berries and sugar in water very slowly until well done. Put through a sieve, you could use a colander just sit it over a bowl mash it thru. When cool add lemon juice. Pour in a big bowl and put in freezer. Freeze until it's thick hard mush. Remove and beat with an electric beater until light and fluffy. Freeze again to a hard mush, then remove and beat with mixer again (all this freezing and mixing keeps ice crystals from forming). Now it's done, store in cartons in the freezer and keep frozen until ready to serve. The secret of this recipe is to mix it 3 or 4 times.

This has been a tradition in my family since 1903 when my great-grandmother Jenny Hunter served it at her China wedding anniversary. I love to make sherbert and I also love to eat it. I have also made this with strawberries, blackberries, raspberries, and pineapple. These fruits don't take as much honey as cranberries do; I'd say you'll only need about 1/4 to 1/2 cup sweetener. You can also use soy or buttermilk for 1/2 the amount of liquid in all sherberts but the cranberry.

This is a delightful dessert and quite a surprise. It is a MUST with any big Thanksgiving or Christmas to-do.

You've also heard me mention Lakewood Peaches and Cream, Strawberries and Cream, coconut milk, and lots of others—all dairyless. These are great to use as half the liquid in any sherbert. They also work in coconut cream pie, banana pudding, or in any icing.

PRISSY'S EASY PEACH COBBLER

1/4 cup margarine
1 cup unbleached white or whole wheat flour
3/4 cup honey
pinch salt
1 TBS. baking powder
2/3 cup milk or soy milk or Lakewood Peaches and Cream
5 cups fresh peaches, sliced (or enough to generously cover the pan)
grated fresh lemon peel
1/4 tsp. cinnamon
1/4 tsp. cloves

This cobbler is the greatest! You assemble it in layers without stirring and the batter poofs up and makes a golden brown topping.

Melt margarine and pour into an oblong casserole dish or what have you. Mix the dry ingredients together and add liquid and honey. Stir up really well. Pour as is, into casserole dish. Remember—don't stir this. Add sliced peaches and any juice they've rendered. I'll tell you again, don't stir this!

With the fine edge of your grater, grate a little lemon peel over it. Sprinkle cinnamon and cloves—just barely. Then bake in a preheated 350^ oven for 40 minutes, or until the top is golden brown. After you have made this once, you'll see why it's the only cobbler recipe I ever use. It also works on most any fruit; I've used berries, apples, blueberries, etc. Fresh-frozen fruit will also do in a pinch.

Seven Layer Cookies

Magic Cookie Bars

Whenever people sit around and talk about their favorite sweet thing, somebody will bring this one up. It is one of the easiest and one of the most loved.

1 stick butter or margarine
1 1/2 cups (1 pack) graham cracker crumbs
1 can Eagle brand milk
1 cup chopped nuts, walnuts for one
1 cup (small package) semi-sweet chocolate chips
1 cup shredded coconut

This is real easy and done in layers—don't stir it up! Melt margarine and pour in 9 by 13 inch pan. Spread graham cracker crumbs next, then nuts, chocolate chips, and coconut last. Pour the Eagle brand milk over the whole thing (I've used milk thickened with corn starch and lots of honey before). Cook in oven at 350^ for 30 minutes. Let cool and cut into squares. Make them small—these are intense and very addictive. Tina likes to keep hers in the refrigerator.

War Cake
Eggless, Butterless AND Milkless

I got this recipe from an old cookbook put out by a Ladies Trinity Mission. The recipe dates back to the Civil War and was not given away, but sold for ten cents to benefit the Red Cross. I have given the original recipe and my own slight variations. I love old recipes like this one! It reminds me of something that Miss Mellie Hamilton would serve at the weekly meeting of the Association for the Beautification of the Graves of Our Glorious Dead.

2 cups brown sugar (I use 1 1/2 cups honey)
2 cups hot water
2 tsp. lard (I use margarine or corn oil)
1 pkg. sultana raisins (I use however many I have around)
1 tsp. salt
1 tsp. cinnamon
1 tsp. cloves

Bring these ingredients to a boil, and continue to cook for 5 minutes. When cool add:

3 cups flour
1 tsp. soda dissolved in a tiny bit of hot water

Bake 45 minutes in a slow oven. I use about 300^. This cake improves by keeping (when it's cooled, wrap in aluminium foil).

AGAR-AGAR

The first time I ever heard of this stuff, I thought, "I may be dumb, but I'm not stupid...it'll be a long time before I make anything to eat out of something called agar-agar." After I saw what it looked like, that made it even easier to ignore. I mean really, long sticks of seaweed? Agar-agar? Jello? No way. I went on stubbornly for years.

One day this girl wandered into the kitchen and said, "Hey, like, uh—I've got some extra time and like, how about swapping some work now for some lunch later?"

She knew her way around the kitchen pretty well, and we hit it right off; moon in Gemini, Venus in Cancer. Things were going great, we were rolling pizza dough when she said, "Hey, like let's do agar for dessert..."

I looked up, stunned—she had seemed like such a nice girl. I knew my time was up; no more excuses. "Okay, just exactly what is this stuff anyway?"

"Later, of course, I couldn't believe I'd gone for so long without taking advantage of this amazing food. It's a perfect natural gelatin—tasteless, dissolves completely and quickly, and some companies have started packaging it in flakes instead of bars for easy measuring.

1 jar (4 cups) Lakewood Peaches and Cream or Lakewood Strawberries and Cream (If you have never seen this juice at your store, then ask for it. It's pretty easily available and very good. It makes the best desserts and it's made with coconut milk, not cow's milk. You would never believe it cause it's so rich.)

2 bars agar-agar or 1 cup agar flakes (read label for your proportions to make sure)
1 tsp. vanilla
1 cup sliced peaches (or strawberries, whichever juice you're using)

Pour the juice into a sauce pan and let it come to a slow boil. If you are using flakes, put them in. If you are using bars, run them under water till they are soft and just put them in the pot. Stir until dissolved. Turn down and simmer about 15 minutes. Add vanilla and the sliced fruit (you just want it to bleed a little). Pour into custard dishes, or a pie plate. Chill till firm (about 2 hours).

Can you believe that's all there is to it? It really is so easy, and it tastes good—believe me. Once you've tried it you won't be able to stop, ideas will pop into your head like crazy.

Old Fashioned Gingerbread

At heart, I'm a chocolate-aholic. I am making a consorted effort to get off white sugar once and for all. In the meantime, when I need something so sweet that it makes my teeth hurt, I make gingerbread. This recipe is so great—no brown sugar, no honey, just one cup of molasses. As soon as Fall comes and there's a little bite in the air, I'm subjected to a primal urge that forces me to leave work early, go home, and make gingerbread. God, the smell of it! And it's so easy. I like it hot right out of the oven, slathered in butter. Steven eats his with a big piece of sweet potato pie; amazingly enough he calls this "a la mode." With apple sauce it makes a great afternoon snack or with hot lemon-honey sauce drizzled over the top it makes a killer midnight snack. This recipe is so easy. What's stopping you?

1 cup whole wheat flour
1/2 cup oats
1/2 tsp. baking soda
1 round TBS. ground ginger
1 tsp. cinnamon
1/4 tsp. allspice
1 stick margarine or 1/2 cup corn oil
or vegatable oil
1 cup unsulfered molasses (dark or light, not
black strap)
2 eggs or egg replacer
2 tsp. vanilla
1/2 cup soymilk
1 big handful raisins
2 big handfuls walnuts or pecans, chopped

This is one of the few recipes that I use an electric mixer on. If you have one, they work great; if you don't, doing it by hand works just as good. Mix all the dry ingredients in a bowl. Cream butter or oil, molasses, eggs or replacer, vanilla, and soymilk. Add dry ingredients and mix well. Now add raisins and nuts and give another quick stir. Pour into buttered pan. I use my glass pie plate and it works great. Bake at 350^ for 35 to 40 minutes. Use a toothpick to test. You may have to run a knife around the edges to get it out smoothly. Enjoy!

MINI✶HA✶HA✶CAKE

1 1/4 to 1 1/2 cups applesauce (or a bit less apple juice)
3/4 cup oats
1/2 cup margarine
1 egg or egg replacer
1 1/2 cup unbleached white flour
2 tsp. baking soda
1/2 to 3/4 cup honey (you could also use any mixture of molasses, brown sugar, or malt)
1 tsp. vanilla
1 tsp. cinnamon
1/2 tsp. ginger

Heat applesauce or juice and pour over oats. Let sit about 15 minutes.

Mix the dry ingredients together. Cream the margarine, honey, egg (or replacer), and spices. Next stir in applesauce and oats, then dry ingredients. Pour into a greased pie plate. Bake at about 375^ for about 40 minutes or till a straw comes out clean. Let it cool a bit and add icing (it is the icing that makes this a mini*ha*ha cake).

FROSTING

2 cups brown sugar or 1 cup brown sugar/1 cup honey
1 cup water
1 1/2 tsp. vanilla
2 eggs or egg replacers
pinch cream of tartar
3/4 cup raisins, chopped
3/4 cup chopped, toasted nuts

Over medium to medium-high heat cook the water and sweetener till it spins a thread. If that sounds weird, it means until it comes off the spoon when lifted in a line about the size of a thread. Stir in very quickly the egg (or replacer), vanilla, and cream of tartar. When smooth, add chopped nuts and raisins and spread on top of cake. That's it.

The icing is good on almost any kind of cake, but I like it on this apple cake the best.

153

There's a Right Way to do Everything

1 cup oats
1/2 cup whole wheat flour
1/2 cup unbleached white flour
1 stick butter
1 tsp. baking powder
1/2 tsp. baking soda
1/2 tsp. salt
3 to 4 heaping TBS. cocoa or carob powder
1 tsp. vanilla
3/4 cup molasses (leave this in cup and
add enough brown sugar to loosely make
1 uneven cup)
1 egg or egg replacer
1 cup roasted almonds, cut coarsely
into big chunks

Chocolate Almond Cookies

To me, nothing tastes better together than chocolate and roasted almonds. I haven't had Swiss chocolate almond ice cream in years and hopefully I have put an end to my addiction to Hershey's chocolate almond bars. What's a girl to do?

One afternoon in a chocolate panic, I invented these cookies; they truly hit the spot.

***If your almonds aren't roasted, pop them into the oven while it's preheating. They can roast while you are mixing other ingredients.
Mix dry ingredients into medium sized bowl. Preheat oven to 350^. Cream butter, molasses and sugar, egg, and vanilla by hand or mixer until smooth. Add dry ingredients, mix well and add nuts. Drop small to medium sized spoonfuls onto greased cookie sheet. Bake about 10 minutes. Let cool enough so that they do not instantly burn your tongue off and enjoy immediately. They are serious winners!

HOUSEHOLD HINTS

HOMEMADE SIN

The only way to do it,
is to start from scratch;
All true what you've heard,
it's a mighty hot batch;
Anything you like,
just put it right on in,
Cause what we're makin' here,
is homemade sin.

You can start early in the morning,
you can let it cook all night;
Stir it around with your fingers,
then lick and take a bite;
No it just don't matter,
if it's yang or if it's yin,
Cause what we're makin' here,
is homemade sin.

Don't bring no cookbook,
you won't need no special recipe;
Just tell them at the kitchen door,
you're comin' to see me,
Our whole world will start to spin,
let's zoom off to oblivion,
It's way over time,
for some homemade sin.

CHORUS
There's only one rule,
so you better listen...
If you can't take the heat,
then get out of the kitchen.

HOUSEHOLD HINTS

NO 1

If you want to test any pasta to see if it's done, take a noodle out with a fork and fling it against the wall. If it sticks, it's done.

NO 2

To keep bugs out of opened bags of grains, put one or two Bay Leaves into the bags after opening them or just keep it in the fridge.

NO 3

What if your husband has his hands around your throat when your dinner guests arrive? The situation is hopelessly beyond your control—there's not really anything you can do anyway, right? (Let's hope your husband is enough of a gentleman to let go of you and answer the door. Take this turn of events as a chance to stop fighting—say you're sorry or let him tell you.) Don't let a silly argument spoil a good evening. These people are your friends, they understand. I've never trusted a girl who didn't have a fight with her man every once and a while. You have a wonderful dinner prepared, so go ahead and enjoy it.

NO 4

My friend Big Bird told me this one. When you don't have any bread crumbs, take a package of crackers and put them in a brown paper bag. Roll the top down loosely. Go outside and put the bag under the tire of your car and drive over it a couple of times. This works fast and makes good crumbs.

NO 5

Grease your muffin tins, bread pans, cookie sheets, etc. with liquid lecithin. This works better than anything I have ever used before. When you turn your muffin tins upside down, the muffins almost fall out. It doesn't leave a funny taste either.

If your hemmoroids pop out, put a dab of liquid lecthin on it for dramatic results.

NO 6

When you're cooking beans, never add the salt until the end of the cooking time. The salt makes the beans constrict and they take 10 times longer to get done.

№ 7

You can make your own rice flour in the blender in minutes. Just add the rice and blend until very fine. Millet works well too. Both are nice roasted first, but you don't have to.

№ 8

Remember, don't put the pies in the oven on top of the rolls. Once, at a pretty wild Thanksgiving dinner, Tina didn't look—she just threw the pie into the oven right on top of a whole pan of refrigerator rolls. The rolls rose and cooked right around the pie. Everything ended up tasting great, but after everyone in the kitchen looked at the pie in the middle of the rolls, we all laughed so hard dinner was delayed at least 20 minutes.

№ 9

Never throw away sour milk. Use it in any recipe that calls for buttermilk (cornbread, hushpuppies, chocolate cake).

№ 10

Leave tomatoes in the window a couple of days before you eat them. This really helps store bought tomatoes and takes away the mealy taste.

№ 11

To ripen an avocado, wrap it in a brown paper bag and put it on top of the refrigerator for a few days.

№ 12

"A little honey in anything savory, A little salt in anything sweet"-From a 100 year old cookbook

№ 13

When you burn the bottom of a pan, wash it as best you can. Then put in about 2 inches of water and 2 or 3 TBS. of baking soda. Let this simmer for awhile. Be careful not to burn it again. You will be completely amazed. If this doesn't work, throw the pot out.

№ 14

If you don't have a biscuit cutter, use a coffee cup or wide mouthed jar.

№ 15

What if the oven blows up in your face? This can be hectic. This is also the reason that good cooks have an aloe vera plant around the house. Cut a frond off the plant, split it open, and press directly and firmly to your face or wherever you are burned. After a while if it doesn't seem as juicy anymore, make some little slashes in it with a knife; this will help render its juices. This works miracles on burns. Try not to let the experience scare you. Go right back into the kitchen—otherwise, you may never bake another apple pie for as long as you live.

№ 16

The most important tool anyone can have in the kitchen is a SHARP knife that really feels right in your hand.

№ 17

I know you already know this one, but it is so important that I'm going to say it anyway. Never throw away water that you use to steam vegetables. It works so well for the liquid in sauces, soups, salad dressings, marinades, absorbed into TVP, etc. Try cooking your rice in vegetable broth instead of plain water.

№ 18

I always put my herbs and spices in to cook first, with the oil and onions, if I'm using them. This seems to bring out something more from them than adding then later.

№ 19

Recipe for coffee:
> "Black as the Devil,
> Hot as Hell,
> Pure as an angel,
> Sweet as Love."
> Charles Talleyrnak-Perigord 1754-1838

№ 20

What if your husband gets bitten on the lip by a dog at your brother's wedding party? Look at it this way: Some ancient form of acupuncture was probably taking place. Maybe he was just saved from a heart attack or an acute appendicitis.

№ 21

Do you know how to care for cast iron? First of all, you can get beautiful pieces at most hardware stores or army surplus. The new ones need to be seasoned just like the old ones you might buy used. They will take a little more elbow grease just to make sure they are clean.

First, scrub it good with steel wool; even old rusty ones will clean right up. This is the ONLY time you should ever use soap on your cast iron. Rinse it well and dry it off. Cover the whole thing, top, bottom, and handle, with a generous coating of oil. Put it in a slow oven, about 100° or so, for at least the whole day. Some people say you can do this for a week. I always pick a good cold day when I don't mind having the oven on all day. Use strictly for frying and sauteing for a while...not steaming or boiling.

Now about everyday cleaning. Wiping with a paper towel should be more than sufficient. If you feel like it needs a little bit more of a cleaning just use a scrubbie, hot water, and some elbow grease; NO SOAP! Always dry your cast iron immediately. Put on a burner over low heat, brush with a little oil when dry (if needed). This will help keep your skillet seasoned. Don't ever store leftovers in cast iron.

These seasoning instructions are ditto for breaking in a wok. Another way of seasoning a wok is to make a lot of popcorn in it. The cleaning, drying, and caring information is also the same.

№ 22

When you are measuring grains for cooking and there's no measuring cup around to measure the liquid, use this fool-proof method: Put the grain in the pan. Point your index finger down until the very tip is touching the top of the grain. Now, add water until it comes to the joint line of your first knuckle.

№ 23

Know when to leave well enough alone. It is easy to get carried away and ruin a perfectly good dinner by worrying over it. Don't doubt the food, just let it do it's thing—you are only the assistant. If you feel like making something wild and adding every spice in the kitchen, then make chutney. If you want to stand over something and stir, make gravy or sesame salt.

№ 24

Too many cooks will curdle the sauce.

№ 25

After you have cut a watermelon, and don't want the end to dry out in the refrigerator, cover the end with a shower cap.

№ 26

"Razors pain you;
Rivers are damp;
Acids stain you;
And drugs cause cramp;
Guns aren't lawful;
Nooses give;
Gas smells awful;
You might as well live."
Dorothy Parker 1893-1967

WHAT IS THIS STUFF ANYWAY??

№ 1 Toasted Sesame oil-- This is a must for vegetarian, southern cooking. This will duplicate the taste of fat back, bacon fat, salt pork and plain old lard that is essential in Southern cooking. Throughout this book if I refer to sesame oil, that is what I mean. You won't need more than a few teaspoons or tablespoons as this flavor is strong.

№ 2 Electric Skillet--If you don't have one, run on out to K-mart and get you one. Fried chicken tofu is just not the same if not made in an electric skillet. It works well for all tofu, tempeh, tvp or seitan dishes that you want to really get a crispy or browned edge.

№ 3 Good Tasting Nutritional Yeast-- Yes, you have to make sure you get the right yeast. There really is a bad tasting one. You want Nutritional Yeast Flakes. Not bakers yeast, or protein powder yeast.

№ 4 Tahini--No, this is not a tropical island. This is ground up sesame seeds. Like peanut-butter only sesame seeds.

№ 5 Miso-- fermented soy bean paste with miracle healing powers. It has a live bacteria like yogurt so when using don't let come to a boil, you'll kill the good stuff.

№ 6 umboshi plums--salted plums that are a great seasoning for soups. They can impart that good old salt pork taste. You can pull the meat off the plum and use that or throw in the whole plum and let cook like that.

INDEX

163

Heart of the Home
is available in bookstores nationwide,
online or send $12 including shipping to
HEART OF THE HOME

c/o

ANN JACKSON
PO Box 679
Snow Camp, NC 27349

also by
ANN JACKSON
COOKIN' SOUTHERN VEGETARIAN STYLE